Successfully
In A Week

Mo Shapiro

Mo Shapiro, partner of INFORM T&C, is a master practitioner in NLP and coaching. She has an outstanding record as a communications and presentation skills coach and trainer and an international public speaker. Mo contributes regularly to all broadcast media, has authored *Neuro-linguistic Programming* and co-authored *Tackling Interview Questions* and *Succeeding at Interviews* in this series.

Teach® Yourself

Interviewing People Successfully

Mo Shapiro

www.inaweek.co.uk

Hodder Education

338 Euston Road, London NW1 3BH.

Hodder Education is an Hachette UK company

First published in UK 1993 by Hodder Education

First published in US 2012 by The McGraw-Hill Companies, Inc.

This edition published 2012

Copyright © 1993, 1999, 2012 Mo Shapiro

The moral rights of the author have been asserted

Database right Hodder Education (makers)

The *Teach Yourself* name is a registered trademark of Hachette UK.

British Library Cataloguing in Publication Data: a catalogue record for this title is available from the British Library.

Library of Congress Catalog Card Number: on file.

The publisher has used its best endeavours to ensure that any website addresses referred to in this book are correct and active at the time of going to press. However, the publisher and the author have no responsibility for the websites and can make no guarantee that a site will remain live or that the content will remain relevant, decent or appropriate.

The publisher has made every effort to mark as such all words which it believes to be trademarks. The publisher should also like to make it clear that the presence of a word in the book, whether marked or unmarked, in no way affects its legal status as a trademark.

Every reasonable effort has been made by the publisher to trace the copyright holders of material in this book. Any errors or omissions should be notified in writing to the publisher, who will endeavour to rectify the situation for any reprints and future editions.

Hachette UK's policy is to use papers that are natural, renewable and recyclable products and made from wood grown in sustainable forests. The logging and manufacturing processes are expected to conform to the environmental regulations of the country of origin.

www.hoddereducation.co.uk

Typeset by Cenveo Publisher Services

Printed in Great Britain by CPI Cox & Wyman, Reading

Contents

Introduction

Interviewing is an integral part of managing people. Many different interviews happen throughout your working day, some are planned and others more spontaneous. *Interviewing People Successfully In A Week* is designed to help you feel prepared for all the interviews you have to conduct. The seven days will give you an insight into the way successful interviews are created as we examine interviewing in detail. Sunday and Monday concentrate on some general interviewing guidelines and techniques while Tuesday to Saturday overview some specific types of interview you may be expected to implement. You are more likely to be involved in selection, appraisal and coaching interviews which are covered on Tuesday, Wednesday and Thursday. Friday's counselling and Saturday's disciplinary interviews will occur less often.

Successful interviewing doesn't just happen, it requires planning and preparation. What goes on during the interview is only part of a continuing process. The greater your preparation, the more confident you'll feel as you go into your interview and this will enable you to focus better on your interviewee and how they are feeling.

Even with the most advanced technology there is a preference to hold interviews in one room wherever possible. People still travel the world in order to have face to face discussions even though they can see and speak to their colleagues via their computer or phone. Using a webcam limits how much body language you can take in and doesn't give you an overall picture (literally and metaphorically) of the person you are interviewing. That said, video interviews and meetings have a place in modern management and are excellent for quickly dealing with urgent issues that can't wait until you 'get there'.

It may be that to date most of your experience has been on the receiving end as the interviewee. We all expect and accept that interviewees can be nervous and worried about the impression they will make and you will see from the companion books *Succeeding at Interviews* and *Tackling Interview Questions* that there is plenty of help provided for them. *Interviewing People Successfully* is designed to redress the balance and acknowledge that interviewers can also feel nervous and unsure about their interviews. After all, you are in charge of the process and have the responsibility to make the 'right' decision or change somebody's behaviour.

I would encourage you to make good use of your interviewee experiences and let them inform how you run your interviews as interviewer. Think about interviewers who you would consider successful when they interviewed you. What did they do and say to make you feel comfortable and able to show yourself in a good light? What can you learn from them and introduce into your own interviewing practice? Remember your interviewee experiences in each type of interview as you go through the days of the week:

Sunday – Discover the four Ps of interviewing

Monday – General skills to give you increased confidence

Tuesday – Key ingredients for a successful selection interview

Wednesday – Making appraisals enjoyable and part of your everyday management

Thursday – Recognize opportunities for coaching to enhance staff performance

Friday – Basic counselling skills

Saturday – Clarifying procedures for disciplinary interviews

SUNDAY

Discover the four Ps of interviewing

Throughout the week we will be considering some of the interviews that you may be conducting as part of your work. Before examining each specific type of interview, there are some basic guidelines that relate to interviews in general.

In considering the four Ps of interviewing, we will cover:

Purpose
Preparation
Performance
Postscripts

The four Ps are designed to be used sequentially wherever possible, though you may not always be able to use them in this linear way. Used in order, the four Ps enable you to check that you have considered your objectives for the interview – what do you want and hope to have happen? From this you can decide what information or paperwork you need, and can start thinking about ways of gathering and imparting the data. Then you are ready to perform, to conduct the interview. Your final task is to review how the interview went, what actions you have committed to and what you have learned from the session.

The four Ps form a handy structure and foundation for any interview. They will help you to clarify where you want to go with the interview, whether you get there and where to go next.

Purpose

Before you proceed, it is advisable to think through the purpose of each interview. If it is not obvious to you why you are interviewing someone then you can guarantee it won't be clear to them either. Even when the interview is spontaneous you can still take time between you to check the purpose and whether there is an expected outcome.

Purpose of the interview
- why interview?
- clear objectives

Why interview?

Emails, letters, tests and reports are fine for disseminating the data one way but an interview provides a dynamic and personal interchange. Whenever you want a flow of information, an interview can be the most effective way of ensuring understanding and a sense of rapport between both parties.

Clear objectives

If you don't know where you are going, you may well end up somewhere else.

Once you have decided that an interview is the most productive way to proceed then you need to have a clear idea of what you are hoping to achieve from it. This will help you decide what preparation is required, the structure you want to follow and how to assess your level of success afterwards. For example, before an appraisal interview, your objectives might be:

Appraisal - Sue Green

Objectives
- joint review of year's performance
- set objectives for next year
- agreed areas for development
- relationships with John and Peter
- training or coaching needs

It is vital to let the interviewee know the objectives too. That way, they can prepare appropriately and be clearer about the type of information you require. It is easy to assume that because you have given great thought to your objectives they will also be obvious to the interviewee. Not so! Interviewees are not mind readers.

It is also important to check what the interviewee's objectives are if you want the interview to be a truly productive and two-way exchange.

AHA!

Preparation

Fail to prepare... Prepare to fail.

Preparation is the key to successful interviewing. This need not be a lengthy process to be valuable. As you become more experienced with different types of interview, you will find that a pattern of preparation emerges and you will develop your own strategy.

Self

You may feel uncertain or nervous about the interview you are about to hold, especially if you are not very practised. It is worthwhile to reflect briefly how you can talk yourself into or out of a successful interview.

Compare...

- **thoughts** I know I'll make a mess of this interview; I could never interview as well as Harry.
- **feelings** Nervous, uncomfortable, panic, inadequate.
- **outcome** Dry mouth, stumbling over words, incompetent impression, avoid interviews.

with...

- **thoughts** I've prepared well for this interview; I'm developing my own interviewing style.
- **feelings** Calm, confident, ready, healthy nerves.
- **outcome** Well-paced interview, interviewee comfortable, positive impression.

Positive self-talk is recognized as a way of enhancing performance whether it be in an interview or on the sports field. If you can direct your energy away from worrying about a situation and towards effective preparation, then you will be creating opportunities for success. When the interview is not as effective or doesn't go to plan, you can use positive self-talk to assist learning rather than beating yourself up for not being perfect. Consider: nobody's perfect...but who wants to be nobody?

Take some steps to relax immediately before the interview. Prepare for success.

Documentation

You need to collect and read through a variety of paperwork before the interview. In the case of selection, appraisal, coaching and discipline interviews you will have a good idea of the data required. Make a list of all the documents needed and if time is short you can prioritize your reading.

● What key questions arise from your reading?
● Where do you want to start the interview?
● What evidence is available to support your argument?
● Which areas do you want to focus on?

Organization

The organizational preparation for an interview fits into three categories: interview structure, scene setting and administrative arrangements.

Interview structure

Having decided the purpose of the interview and reviewed the relevant documentation, the next step is to consider the

SUNDAY
MONDAY
TUESDAY
WEDNESDAY
THURSDAY
FRIDAY
SATURDAY

structure. You can mentally plan or write down your opening words and jot down the stages you intend to follow:

- before interview – schedule enough time in your diary; inform interviewee of location; set out interview plan
- during interview – establish rapport; agree or state objectives, set agenda; stick to the point; develop theme(s); summarize and agree conclusions/actions; plan next step/ arrange next interview; close clearly
- after interview – review the content; review the process; follow up agreed actions. What worked well and what might you do differently next time?

Scene setting

The location of the room and the way it is set out can significantly affect the interview process. You will require somewhere quiet, free from interruptions (whether from phones, PDAs, laptops or other people) and with enough space not to feel cluttered or crowded. Make sure that you and the interviewee(s) turn off your phones and close your laptops. It is disrespectful, distracting and off-putting not to do so.

You need to find a balance in the room between distractions like paintings, posters, ostentatious ornaments and 'executive toys' and somewhere too sterile, which will be cold and unwelcoming.

If you are holding a panel interview with a number of interviewers, you need to set the room out so that the interviewee feels comfortable and unthreatened.

What seating arrangements can you make? Both the formality of the interview and the space available to you may determine this. The room layout is one of the first things the interviewee will notice. It is a good idea for most interviews to place yourself on the same side of the desk as the interviewee. If you have chairs set around a coffee table, make sure there is room for you both to have papers and somewhere to put a drink. This way there is no barrier between you and the interviewee and no sense of suggesting that you are the more important person.

Sitting behind a desk can suggest that you are inaccessible, too busy or even frightened by the interviewee. In some offices, you will have no choice about the desk. If this is the case, you should at least make sure that the chairs are at the same height and that the desk is free from clutter and distractions.

Administrative arrangements

● When is the best time for the interview?
Late morning/midday if the interviewee has to travel. End of the day for counselling or discipline.

● How can you block interruptions?
Turn off phones, pagers and laptops and put an 'engaged' or 'do not disturb' notice outside the door. Use an office away from yours, preferably a designated meeting room.

● How many interviews should be held in a day?
If they are going to be longer than 15 minutes, you should try to stop at six a day. Any more and the early ones will be forgotten, and your performance will be impaired in the final ones.

Performance

You can now go into the interview confident that you have set clear objectives, read the necessary documentation, decided the interview structure and set the room out to your liking. The next step is to manage the interview itself. Think about the points below.

Interview style

A warm and non-threatening opening to the interview will enhance whatever style you then go on to use. The main essence of the interview is to establish a rapport with your interviewee to settle them down. Then you can use one or more of the following interview styles.

Joint problem-solving

Here, concentrate on a particular problem, settle together on a way round it and get the interviewee's commitment to the agreed goals and actions.

Tell – listen

Provide the interviewee with relevant information or with your assessment of the situation under discussion, and then listen to their ideas for action.

Tell – sell

This assumes that you know best! You state the facts and then sell your solution to the interviewee. The danger is that the interviewee will not be committed to your goal.

Listen – support

There may be no 'solution' in this kind of interview. Your role is to allow the interviewee to work through their concerns and consider different ways of managing these.

Taking notes

In most interviews, it is wise to take brief notes to supplement the detailed information that your company requires.

Notes are not recommended for a counselling interview where the emphasis is on confidentiality. In any case, you will want to use all your concentration to listen wholeheartedly to the interviewee.

One of the main problems with notes is the distraction caused by the break in eye contact with the interviewee while you are writing.

Hints for note-taking

- Tell the interviewee you're planning to take notes and suggest that he or she does too.
- Keep notes short and to the point.
- Put the interviewee's words between quotation marks.
- Write up notes straight after interview.
- Note facts not personal information.

Prejudice and bias

It is crucial to remember that you can make decisions about a person or the outcome of an interview in a very short time. Where that is the case, you need to check whether you are relying on 'instincts' or assumptions rather than the facts. If you are selecting a candidate with whom you will be working closely, it is appropriate to pay attention to your gut feelings about them. You can also consider the source of these responses. The interviewee's appearance, someone else's opinion or the fact they arrived early or late may have influenced you unfairly.

When you are conducting an interview with someone you know well, unsubstantiated information may also be influential. If you are inclined against an interviewee, you may only notice interactions that reinforce that view. On the other hand, a particular piece of work may so impress you that you only see the positive side of that interviewee when there might also be areas for improvement. Either way, your prejudices can lead to an outcome that you predicted and subconsciously encouraged. Concentrate on the whole picture, not just the parts that impress or disappoint you.

Be wary too of your prejudices landing you in trouble with racial or sexual discrimination and sexual harassment. Many companies have their own codes of practice and provide equal opportunities training. If you are to be involved in much interviewing, it is advisable to make yourself familiar with these codes and with the law on such matters.

Postscripts

The three important post interview activities are: writing up the notes, following-up agreed actions and self-assessment.

Writing up the notes

As soon as the interviewee has departed, write out your notes in full. This may mean filling in a company form or a record card. Don't leave it until later. Once you are back in the swing of work, the notes probably won't make sense.

Following-up agreed actions

If you have agreed to find some information, talk to a colleague, set up a meeting or contact a client, then start to draw up a plan for yourself. How much time do you need to commit to the action? Who else is involved? When is your deadline? What is your review date? Take care that you haven't landed yourself with more actions than your interviewee. Of course you will have some actions and do encourage them to take responsibility too.

Review and self-assessment

Give yourself time to go back over the interview and assess your performance. Was the outcome satisfactory? Was your preparation appropriate?

Some self-assessment questions

- Did I establish a rapport from the start?
- Did I clearly state my agenda and objectives?
- Did we agree a shared agenda and objectives?
- Did I listen fully to their discourse?
- Did I summarize accurately?
- Did I follow my interview plan? If not, was that appropriate?
- Did we reach a consensus for future action?
- Did we both gain from the interview?
- What will I do differently next time?
- What worked well and will I do more of?

Summary

Today's guidelines will stand you in good stead whatever type of interviews you are called upon to conduct. Remembering the four Ps will provide you with a checklist of what you need to do and when to do it. I would be delighted if you create your own checklist and reminders that help you feel confident as an interviewer and increase the ease with which absorb the main points. A few questions might help you to do this.

- What type of interviews do you conduct most often?
- What do you like least about interviewing?
- What do you like most about interviewing?
- How can you use and embellish the four Ps to customize them for your own use?

You may find one or two of the four Ps easier than the others and this in itself could be an indication of where your interviewing limitations and strengths lie. Are you happier preparing or performing? Do you mostly have clear objectives for your interviews and let yourself down when it comes to reviewing and evaluating what happened?

Tomorrow takes a detailed look at the performance side of the interview and considers the key generic skills you might want to utilize.

SUNDAY

MONDAY

TUESDAY

WEDNESDAY

THURSDAY

FRIDAY

SATURDAY

Questions (answers at the back)

1. The advantages of face-to-face interviews are:
   a) You get the full picture of body language ❏
   b) It's harder for the interviewee to lie ❏
   c) You can better assess the other person's motivation ❏
   d) You feel more in control of the interview ❏

2. The four Ps of interviewing include:
   a) Performance ❏
   b) Prevarication ❏
   c) Preparation ❏
   d) Posture ❏

3. You need clear objectives for your interviews to:
   a) Assist with your preparation and data collection ❏
   b) Help interviewees know what to expect ❏
   c) Evaluate your success ❏
   d) Make sure that they are the same as the interviewees' ❏

4. When preparing yourself for an interview with positive self-talk, you:
   a) Feel confident ❏
   b) Expect to fail ❏
   c) Have a greater chance of success ❏
   d) Ensure a positive start ❏

5. When thinking about the interview structure:
   a) Mentally plan or record your opening words ❏
   b) Be sure to have considered your actions before, during and afterwards ❏
   c) Plan minute by minute ❏
   d) Warn the interviewee that they will have to review the process ❏

6. When preparing the location of the interview, do you:
   a) Hope a room will be free when you need it ❏
   b) Consider and arrange the seating in advance ❏
   c) Be sure to sit behind a desk in a high chair ❏
   d) Consider the set up from the interviewee's perspective ❏

7. When taking notes in an interview:
   a) Give the interviewee advance notice of your intention ❏
   b) Write down everything they say ❏
   c) Record your assumptions as well as factual information ❏
   d) Write longer notes straight after the interview ❏

8. How do you assess an interviewee?
a) On instincts and feelings from first impressions ❑
b) On your prior knowledge of the person ❑
c) On the whole picture accumulated throughout the interview ❑
d) Following equal opportunities guidelines ❑

9. After an interview, it is important to:
a) Tell everyone how the interview went ❑
b) Follow-up agreed actions ❑
c) Ensure that the interviewee enjoyed the interview ❑
d) Review and assess your performance ❑

10. Post interview, questions you might ask yourself include:
a) Did I summarize accurately? ❑
b) Was the interview long enough? ❑
c) Did the interviewee like me? ❑
d) Did I establish rapport from the start? ❑

MONDAY

General interviewing skills

Yesterday you worked through, and possibly designed, your personal structure for before, during and after your interviews. So, the scene is set, you have thought through the basic objectives and your required outcomes for an interview. Now is the time to consider exactly how you might achieve them. There are a number of fundamental skills that go a long way towards creating a successful interview. Many interviews fail simply because the interviewer has not followed a few basic guidelines. Yesterday, I mentioned the importance of establishing rapport with your interviewee. It is most important that both parties feel a positive connection during the interview and it is your task to create this. Rapport is demonstrated in many ways, including active listening and body language. You want the interviewee to know that you are with them and want them to do their best. If you understand that they may be nervous or unsure and can settle them early on in the interview, then they are more likely to feel as relaxed as is possible and able to focus on the interview, rather than their nerves.

In considering generic interviewing skills, we will cover:

Active listening
Questions
Body language
Obstacles

Active listening

This is a key skill in any kind of interview. Effective listening involves a lot more than just not speaking at the same time as someone else; a cardboard cut-out can do that. You have to be active in processing what you hear and responding appropriately. You should expect to be listening much more than speaking. Try using the following skills and you'll see how active listening can be.

Paraphrasing

This is a way of restating as accurately as possible what the other person has said; using your own words to show you have been listening and have understood them. It is very helpful to play back what you hear; you check your understanding and sometimes it helps them to clarify theirs. Paraphrasing aids memory and can instantly prevent misunderstanding.

'So what happened was...'
'You seem to be saying...'
'You're telling me that when you started here you thought you'd be a junior manager in five years and now six years on you don't see any sign of that.'

Clarifying

As well as seeking clarification from the speaker, this skill also underlines the message 'I really want to understand'. It is all too tempting to think you know what someone means or how they feel when the only indication they give is a vague 'you know' or an unfinished sentence. Clarifying enables you to focus on specific detail rather than generalization.

'No I don't. I don't think I do know what you mean...'
'I'm not sure whether it's the status, or having more responsibility that is your major concern.'

Encouragers

These aim to keep the person talking with the minimum input from you. One way is to repeat a word or short phrase exactly as spoken by the other person. This encourages them to say some more about that specific area. It often sounds like a question.

'Junior manager?'
'You enjoy bargaining meetings.'

Another way of encouraging someone is to keep quiet and nod your head or say 'aha', 'mm', 'yes' or 'OK'. The interviewee then carries on talking confident that you are involved.

However, if you use encouragers too often you may find you are not listening, or give the impression of not listening, just responding like a nodding dog.

Silence

Silence is helpful in two ways. First, it means you listen to the end of the sentence rather than butting in when you think you've understood enough. People sometimes need thinking time and the chance to breathe before carrying on. Second, it allows space between what you say and the other's response. It can take time for people to consider what you have said and how it affects them, especially if you have hit a sensitive area.

Summarizing

This is a very useful skill for drawing together what has been said towards the end of a section of discussion or the end of the interview. A summary provides a final check for clarity after you have agreed certain actions or decisions and before you each go your separate ways.

'Let me see if this is right. You're feeling frustrated with your position in the company. You are worried that your work rate is falling dramatically and that seems guaranteed to block any hopes of movement. You're going to keep a record of what you are doing with your time over the next week and I'm going to look out training opportunities for you.'

Questions

Once you have satisfied yourself and the interviewee that you have understood, it is time to gather further information. Obviously, the type of questioning you use will determine what you want to know or discuss next.

Types of question can include:

- open questions
- hypothetical questions
- closed questions
- keep off!

Open questions

Open questions do precisely that and open up an area of enquiry, allowing the interviewee to expand on a subject in the way they choose.

'Tell me some more about...?'
'What ideas do you have?'
'How might that affect your chances of promotion?'

Open questions often start with the words *how*, *what*, *which*, *when*, *where*, *who* or *why*. Watch out when you are asking 'why' questions. Although they are open, they can also seem interrogatory and abrasive. 'Tell me about...' or 'Say some more about...' are both additional, good ways of letting the interviewee answer from their 'world'.

Hypothetical questions

These questions encourage the speaker to use their imagination.

'What's your idea of our most difficult customer?'
'How would you handle them?'
'Where do you see yourself five years from now?'

Similar to brainstorming in training, you can work crazy thoughts into innovative processes in one-to-one interviews. Interviewees need to be clear that you genuinely want to hear their ideas and are not trying to trap them. So take care when using hypothetical questions in selection and recruitment interviews. Candidates may feel under pressure to give you the 'right' answer.

Closed questions

Closed questions invite single word or yes/no answers. They are useful when you want a precise piece of information or when you want to stop someone from waffling on. Use them sparingly; they can close the discussion down before you are ready. Sometimes a closed question will elicit an open answer if it is delivered in a way that suggests you are genuinely interested.

'Did you take responsibility for the accounts when Sally was away?'
'Would you be interested in a sideways move?'

Keep off!

There are several forms of questioning which you should avoid. Don't:

● Ask questions which relate to your interests or satisfy your curiosity.

'This may not seem relevant but I've always been fascinated by your department's publicity...'

● Ask more than one question at a time.

'Would you say your progress so far has been satisfactory? What sorts of promotions have you gone for? Are you thinking about moving on?'

If you get an answer, to which of those will it relate?

● Answer your own question.

'How did you feel when Sue was promoted? Furious I expect.'

● Ask leading questions.

'You wouldn't want to upset anyone like that, would you?'

Body language

It's not just what you say. The way that you say it makes a greater impact than the words themselves. All of the following can affect the outcome of an interview.

● **S**ound
● **H**abits
● **E**ye contact
● **P**osture

Sound

The way you use your voice in interviews can make all the difference to the message you convey. A genuine enquiry into someone's workload can seem like a throwaway line (too quiet), an accusation (too loud), an apology (too rambling) or an unpleasant dig (sarcastic edge).

Habits

Have you ever been so distracted by someone clicking their pen or tapping their fingers that you lose the sense of what they are saying to you? Some of your gestures will be habitual responses whether you are fascinated, bored or pressurized by the interviewee. The problem is that you don't know what you are doing and the other person may misunderstand your intent. Ask your colleagues.

Watch for:

● pointing finger or pen
● hands covering mouth
● inappropriate smile
● foot tapping.

Do your gestures reinforce or contradict your message?

Eye contact

One way to show someone that you are interested in them and what they are saying is to maintain steady eye contact while they are talking. Just five to ten seconds before looking away is enough to demonstrate your attention. Over ten seconds uninterrupted eye contact can start to become intimidating. When your eyes wander, you may give an impression of boredom, fear or insincerity. Notice how you feel when different people look at you or away from you. If you find eye contact difficult, look at the interviewee's forehead or nose. That way you are concentrating on the important area.

Posture

Consider how you sit when you are interviewing. If you have your arms and legs crossed, you will look unreceptive and you are likely to be feeling tense. Open up and you can breathe more freely and communicate accessibility. Lean forward to give yourself more impact.

Think about the space between you and the interviewee. Some people are comfortable sitting closely together while others can feel claustrophobic. Be sensitive to comfort zones.

Obstacles

On Sunday, we looked at organizational hindrances to an effective interview. Below, we consider some *attitudes* that can be hindrances to an effective interview.

Comparing

This is a hindrance because you are likely to be trying to assess whether the interviewee is cleverer than you or more likely to catch the MD's eye. While they are talking, you may be thinking:

'Could she do it as well as me?'
'That's a better idea than any of mine.'

Open ears – closed mind

Sometimes you decide rather quickly that you can predict how the conversation will continue. This may be because you have talked to the person before or, more dangerously, because someone else has 'forewarned' you. You think that there is no reason to concentrate any longer as you will not hear anything new. You may also become selective and only hear the bits that fit in with your preconceptions. The better you think you know someone, the more likely you are to make assumptions in your interview. These are dangerous. You find that you have been following different trains of thought and it will take ages to return to the same track.

Red rag

Each of us can identify words or phrases that cause immediate emotional reactions. Similar to a bull chasing a red rag, we cease listening in order to jump and pounce on the offending statement. Once colleagues have spotted these words, they can use them to take you away from your agenda for the interview.

OH, PARDON!

Distractions

These can be irrelevant thoughts or images that come to the forefront of your mind. (Did you remember to send that email? How are you going to sort out that misunderstanding with accounts? What's for lunch?) You have to practise putting them on hold or making a quick note so as not to be distracted for too long.

Language

Choose your language carefully and adapt it to the interviewee's. Avoid using jargon.

Summary

You probably use many of today's skills already. If there are some that need refreshing or adding to your repertoire, try them out and see what happens at the next interview you hold. Make them part of your planning and only tackle one new skill at a time. Otherwise, your attention will be on techniques and not the interview.

Think about effective interviews you have experienced: What skills were used and what made them work? How did the interviewer put you at ease? What kind of questions hindered or helped you to explain yourself? How did you know they were listening to you and genuinely interested in what you had to say? What have you learned from any ineffective interviews?

Interview skills to remember:

- Listen carefully and actively.
- Leave space for the interviewee to think and reflect on your words
- Encourage them with minimal input.
- Make sure the interviewee has the chance to say what they want.
- Listen until they have finished speaking.
- Keep checking and showing that you understand.
- Regularly paraphrase and summarize what you hear.
- Think about your use of questions.
- Remember SHEP (Sound, Habits, Eye contact, Posture).
- Use all your body to demonstrate your interest and encouragement.
- Don't let your thoughts wander, keep focussed on the interviewee.

Questions (answers at the back)

1. You can create rapport in an interview with:
   a) Body language ❑
   b) Note taking ❑
   c) Active listening ❑
   d) Distractions ❑

2. Active listening in interviews includes:
   a) Moving around ❑
   b) Clarification ❑
   c) Summarizing ❑
   d) Changing location ❑

3. Which of the following are closed questions?
   a) Are you aware of the health and safety policy here? ❑
   b) What can you tell me about the health and safety policy here? ❑
   c) How would you change the health and safety policy here? ❑
   d) Have ever been hindered by the health and safety policy here? ❑

4. When asking questions in an interview don't:
   a) Answer your own question ❑
   b) Wait for a full reply if you know what's coming ❑
   c) Ask more than one question at the same time ❑
   d) Allow thinking space between questions ❑

5. In body language, the mnemonic SHEP stands for:
   a) Speech, Hearing, Examination, Posture ❑
   b) Speech, Habits, Eye Contact, Position ❑
   c) Sound, Habits, Eye Contact, Posture ❑
   d) Sound, Hearing, Examination, Position ❑

6. Regular eye contact throughout an interview demonstrates:
   a) You don't believe what they are saying ❑
   b) You are paying attention to what they are saying ❑
   c) You want to put them under pressure ❑
   d) You are only interested in their responses ❑

7. The way you sit and the space you create in an interview can:
   a) Make you seem tense ❑
   b) Make them feel uncomfortable ❑
   c) Affect their message ❑
   d) Influence the way you are perceived ❑

8. You can avoid prejudice in an interview by:
   a) Not taking other people's opinions into the interview ❑
   b) By only listening to ideas that match yours ❑
   c) Checking out your initial assumptions ❑
   d) Starting with a clean slate ❑

9. You can improve your interviewing skills by:
a) Learning from your experiences as an interviewee ❏
b) Listening to colleagues and noticing what works and you can copy ❏
c) Doing as many interviews as possible ❏
d) Trying lots of new techniques at each interview ❏

10. Successful interviewing skills to remember are:
a) Stay focussed throughout the interview ❏
b) Make sure that you do most of the talking ❏
c) Use mainly closed questions ❏
d) Regularly paraphrase and summarize what you have heard ❏

Selection and recruitment

Having considered some general skills and objectives on Sunday and Monday, today we will look specifically at interviewing for selection and recruitment. It is likely that you and your business will have invested a significant amount of time in the planning process – scoping the role, allocating a budget, talking to the stakeholders, defining the competencies and the person specification, planning the advertisement and briefing headhunters or recruitment consultants, well before the interviewee is actually in front of you. After receiving applications, the tasks are far from over. You, the interviewer, or someone else in the organization, has to arrange the first steps:

- long-listing
- short-listing
- first interviews – sometimes by telephone
- second interviews
- assessments
- meeting the stakeholders.

The interview is part of a larger process and the one that finally determines who will be appointed. So it's important for you to remember your key objectives and questions you are seeking to answer. Can they *do* the job? Do they *match* their CV data? Can they demonstrate that they have the *skills and experience* and do they *fit* your competency needs?

In considering selection interviews, we will look at:

Preparation
The interview
Follow up

Preparation

Preparation, as always, is a most important step in the interview process.

Type of interview

Most recruitment interviews are held between two people: the candidate and the employer/manager. In some cases, a panel is convened with staff from different parts of the organization or departments that have a vacancy. Alternatively, candidates will be called for sequential one-to-one interviews with interested parties to an assessment centre.

A panel will need to meet before the interviews to agree on a chairperson and the areas they each want to cover. It is a good idea to stick to your specific area and not to ask other people's questions. Obviously, it does not look favourable if the panel is competing or squabbling during the interview. The candidate will be assessing you and your organization too.

One drawback of both panel and sequential interviews is that co-ordinating diaries for busy people can be very difficult.

Today we will concentrate on one-to-one interviews.

Purpose

To be able to conduct an effective selection interview, you need to think about your reason for choosing this method of recruitment over any other – for example, personality tests or references.

Gathering information

One reason for the interview is to check that the information received from the candidate on paper, in the form of a CV, letter of application or application form, matches the impression you build up as you go through the interview. You are looking for the best person to do the job and need to find the person with the skills, experience, knowledge and attitude to deliver this.

Matching process

You want to match the candidate as closely as you can to the job description and the person specification. You are also looking for someone who will fit into your particular organization. A charming individual with tons of qualifications but no dress sense will not suit an upmarket design centre.

For each post, think about:

- Are you looking for a certain 'type' of person?
- Are you looking for a specific set of skills?
- If both of the above, then is either more important?

The interviewee also uses the interview to assess how you and the company match their needs and expectations.

Gold discs

Compare personalities

The interview allows you to put together a fuller picture of the interviewees. People can be very hard to separate in terms of paper qualifications and attributes but are very different when seen 'live'. You can use the interview to compare candidates' performances under pressure. This may be key to the appointment.

Interview plan

This is crucial to the success of your interview. Having clarified your objectives, you can now plan how to meet them. You'll feel more confident and relaxed if you have a clear and easy-to-follow format that is the same for all candidates. This also acts as a safeguard against you being led away from your agenda.

Interview plan
- setting the scene
- timing
- your questions
- their questions

Setting the scene

As you saw on Sunday, your organizational preparation for the interviews will make an immediate impression on the candidates. Just as you will make some 'instant' judgements about them, so they will deduce certain things about you.

It is essential to do whatever you can to guarantee *no interruptions*; you may choose to put a notice on the door, transfer phone calls or put phones on silent. If you normally share an office, you need to agree that it can be yours for as long as necessary or arrange to occupy another office.

Some people like to go to a local hotel for guaranteed privacy, but that way they deny candidates the opportunity to look at their potential workplace and sample the atmosphere. They could think you have something to hide.

Timing

Decide a schedule that allows you time to interview, reflect, write notes and prepare for the next person. Most interviews will take between 20 minutes and half an hour. You may need longer for second and panel interviews or when filling senior posts.

It is important to leave yourself a minimum of 10 minutes between each candidate. This gives you time to complete your notes and ideas on the previous applicant and prepare to concentrate on the next. If you plan to drink tea or coffee with candidates, leave yourself space for natural breaks.

If you are running late, then let the waiting candidates know personally or arrange for someone to let them know when they arrive. This signals that you respect the value of their time.

Your questions

Prepare some questions for each candidate before the interview. Depending on their answers, your supplementary questions may well differ. It is important to be consistent with each person. Here are some suggestions:

Opening:

- How was your journey?
- Do you know this area at all?

Main frame:

- Why did you choose to study... at school/college/university?
- Which aspects of your training/education did you enjoy? Not enjoy?
- What made you choose a career in this field?
- You have been working for your present employer for a short/long time. What makes you want to move now?
- How do you think your career to date equips you for this post?
- What strengths could you bring to this job? What limitations might hamper you?

A word of warning. When considering your questions, be familiar with current equal opportunities legislation and your company policy. This also applies to advertising the post and the job descriptions. Check this with the personnel department, HR and senior managers.

During the interview, you should make brief notes of key points. If you have chosen informal seating arrangements, think about using a clipboard or the end of a table to rest your notepad. Remember that you have allowed at least 10 minutes after the interview to compile detailed notes to assist your final decision. Some people choose to score each answer to give a true comparison and this is particularly useful with panel interviews.

Their questions

The candidate may have covered these during the interview. It is still worth checking whether they have anything to ask or to add about themselves. Most interviewees will have prepared questions for the interview. The sorts of questions people ask give you an insight into their priorities, thoughts and attitudes.

Just as you wanted clarification from their written application, they may identify missing information in the data you supplied on your website. Be ready for *job-related* questions like:

- How did the vacancy arise?
- What achievements are you looking for in the first six/twelve months?
- Can you give me a clear picture of what the job involves?

They may ask you to explain more about reporting lines, culture, appraisal and how their performance will be monitored or measured. If you are not the only person responsible for the vacant post, the applicant will want to know who to report to. Be ready for *organizational* questions like:

● How will my work be monitored?
● What are the organization's long-range plans?
● What appraisal system does the company run?
● What opportunities for advancement are there?

If someone is planning to stay with your company, they will be keen to find out about career opportunities. Even if they do not aspire to managerial posts, they will want to know what is available to keep them up to date in their particular field of work. Be ready for *personal development* questions like:

● Could you give me examples of the best results the previous holders of this position have attained?
● What kind of staff development and training programmes do you have?
● How do you determine eligibility for further training?
● Are there opportunities for day-release studies?

HOW DID THE VACANCY ARISE?

The interview

The interview will follow a sequence: an opening stage to settle the applicant and possibly yourself; the main frame; their questions, which have already been covered; and the conclusion.

Opening stage

At this point, you want to outline the structure of the interview and generally put the applicant and yourself at ease. After a general welcome and pleasantries, you may want to say something like:

- I will briefly tell you about the company.
- I would like to clarify some points in your application.
- Then I would like discuss your education and employment history as they relate to this post.
- Finally, I will be pleased to answer any of your questions that haven't been covered.

A logical and stated structure ensures that you both know where you are going. Though you will have some standard, prepared questions for each candidate, they are only guidelines, which will become millstones if you do not allow yourself any flexibility.

Main frame

Is there anything you have highlighted from the written application that needs clarification? Data regarding your candidates will derive from application forms, CVs, letters, personality and numerical tests. You will have re-read these before the interview and highlighted particular areas of interest and concern.

A word of warning. Beware of making assumptions from the written material and then spending the interview trying to prove them right or wrong.

Next, you will want to gain a clear picture of the person's educational and working background. Competence relates to the skills, knowledge and behaviours which, combined, produce the required results. They don't simply focus on *what* someone does, but *how* they do it.

This generally reflects a shift from the concept of education to the concept of learning: from input (classroom-based learning) to outputs (self-paced learning, coaching); from becoming qualified to being fully developed. You will probably ask less about the institutions or courses they've attended, and more about how they have applied their learning. Competencies may also include characteristics such as resilience and influence.

Possible questions relating to these include:

Resilience:

- How do you bounce back after a setback?
- When have you demonstrated resilience?

Influencing:

- Tell me when you persuaded someone senior to do something they were unwilling to do.
- Which areas of influence challenge you most?

You will have used the person specification and job description to help you plan your questions. Build on this information to relate skills and personality to the vacant post. Talk about the vacancy and probe for ideas or possible problem areas.

'Your last three job changes look like sideways moves; how would you see this one?'

Ending

It is your responsibility to signal and close the interview. You may want to summarize where you have reached and what, if any, is the next stage.

'I am interviewing a number of candidates for this post. All interviews will be completed today and I will be able to inform you of the decision by Tuesday next week.'

Check that their expenses have been covered, thank the applicant for their time, stand up and show them out.

Follow up

Here you need to consider what you have told the candidate you will do after the interview. If no one stands out, do not be tempted to appoint the best of a bad lot. You may have to repeat the whole process and spend some extra time and money now rather than saddling the company with second best and generating future problems. Calling a couple of people back for a second interview may be enough to iron out your concerns.

When making your decision, bear in mind the following key points.

Candidate's suitability:

- competencies
- qualifications
- similarities in prior employment
- ability to do the job.

Personality traits:

- initiative
- fit with job description
- fit with person specification.

The candidates will be expecting a decision by whatever time and manner you agreed to contact them. Make sure that you or a representative honour this commitment. Think about giving unsuccessful candidates some feedback and information about their interview. What impressed you and what, if anything, let them down. It may just make the difference for the next time. If you haven't already taken references, this is the time to do so, and any job offer will be subject to these being satisfactory.

Summary

You and your organization want to make the best decision. The amount of investment in terms of time and money (advertising, recruiters/agency costs, etc.) can be immense. It is important that you make the interview as clear and constructive as possible. If this interview is part of an assessment centre, when will you review your findings with other interested parties? Have you thought about how much weight your views and opinions will carry?

There is plenty to think about in selection and recruitment interviews. By preparing fully and deciding your main objectives, you can put all your energy into making the interview highly effective.

Checklist questions

- Are you clear about the job description and person specification?
- Do you know what you are expecting from the candidate?
- Have you checked what are facts and what are assumptions?
- How will you set out the interview room?
- Have you decided and listed your key questions?
- What might the interviewee ask you?
- Is there sufficient breathing space between interviews?

Questions (answers at the back)

1. When planning your selection interview you need to:
   a) Scope the role ❑
   b) Know who you want for the job ❑
   c) Check references ❑
   d) Brief headhunters ❑

2. Your key objectives in a selection interview are:
   a) Do they look the part? ❑
   b) Do they fit your competence needs? ❑
   c) Have you met them before? ❑
   d) Can they match their CV criteria? ❑

3. You want your successful candidate to match:
   a) The CEO's personality ❑
   b) The organization's branding ❑
   c) The person specification ❑
   d) The job description ❑

4. Your interview plan should include:
   a) Setting the scene ❑
   b) Arrival of the tea trolley ❑
   c) Their questions ❑
   d) Timings ❑

5. Your opening questions are designed to:
   a) Settle them down ❑
   b) Dig deep into their CV ❑
   c) Create rapport ❑
   d) Pass the time ❑

6. Their questions are likely to be about:
   a) Reporting lines and performance management ❑
   b) Social opportunities ❑
   c) The organization ❑
   d) The local weather ❑

7. The main frame of your questions is designed to:
   a) Explore common interests ❑
   b) Create a list of their achievements ❑
   c) Clarify data sent to you by the interviewee ❑
   d) Help you understand their skills and knowledge ❑

8. The competencies you might look for include:
   a) Resilience ❑
   b) Influence ❑
   c) Competitiveness ❑
   d) Thoughtfulness ❑

9. As part of your follow up to the selection interview you:
   a) Offer the job without references ❑
   b) Give interviewee feedback, if possible ❑
   c) Contact interviewee when you said you would ❑
   d) Give up and appoint the best of a bad lot ❑

10. Your selection interview checklist covers:

a) Do I know my objectives for the interview? ❏

b) Have I booked a suitable room? ❏

c) Do I want to interview through lunch? ❏

d) Have I created and listed my key questions? ❏

WEDNESDAY

Appraisal

Many managers consider performance appraisals or annual reviews as one of their most disliked tasks. This is not surprising if it is the only time they have a full, forthright discussion with individual staff. Used poorly, performance appraisals become a dreaded annual exercise that is widely seen as a waste of corporate time and resources. When used well, however, the procedure can focus every person's attention on the mission, strategy, vision, and values of the organization. It makes it possible to answer the two questions that every person asks: what do you expect of me, and how am I doing at meeting your expectations? Appraisal differentiates among outstanding, solid and marginal performers.

While performance appraisal is an important part of performance management, in itself it is not performance management; rather, it is one of the range of tools that can be used to manage performance. These include performance development, training, cross-training, challenging assignments, 360-degree feedback and regular performance feedback.

Today we will focus on the appraisal interview which, at its most effective, can *mobilize the energy of every employee toward the achievement of strategic goals.* In many cases, performance appraisals review past actions and behaviour and so provide an opportunity to reflect on past performance. But to be successful, they should also be used as a basis for making development and improvement plans and reaching agreement about what should be done in the future. Remember: an appraisal interview is an opportunity to take the time to overview and plan in an unhurried atmosphere. Both parties need to understand and appreciate that this is an opportunity to exchange ideas, not an excuse for an annual slanging match.

In looking at appraisal interviews, we will focus on:

The purpose
Preparation
The interview
Follow up

The purpose

Be clear about your company's definition and purpose of appraisal interviewing before you embark on any (or any more) staff appraisals. At the very least, an appraisal interview is a regular means of letting employees know how well they are performing in relation to established standards. It also provides the opportunity for them to air their views about their employment. The quality of the discussion is a key to the success of the appraisal process.

Possible purposes of appraisal

The purposes of appraisal include the following:

Organizational:

● conduct a stock-take of potential
● reduce staff turnover
● identify employees' strengths and weaknesses
● provide data for manpower and succession planning
● improve in-company communication.

Managerial:

● improve and extend present performance
● assess development or promotion potential

- set objectives for performance
- discover appraisee's ambitions
- reinforce recognition and support for appraisee's work to date = increased motivation
- obtain information for pay review.

Individual:

- recognize jobs well done
- review performance
- discuss weaknesses and how to improve
- gain commitment for training
- chart possible career progression
- improve morale and increase confidence.

It will help your interview if the organization has policy documents setting out their guidelines and expectations. Is there an appraisal handbook?

You also need to consider who in the company will have access to the content of the interview and whether this is recorded or reported. The appraisee needs to know this too. It will affect what they say during the interview. Be sure to have a private area on your computer that can only be accessed by password.

Performance and pay

Wherever possible, it is a good idea to separate a performance appraisal from a pay review. You want to encourage open and frank discussion with the appraisee. This is much more difficult when they believe that they must show only their successes to be sure of the best pay award. Equally, you may find yourself having to grade the appraisee to fit the monetary amounts available for rewarding good performance. This can lead to you pre-judging a series of interviews to fit your finances. Another advantage of separating the two functions is that following the appraisal, your employee can work on any agreed improvements before the pay review takes place.

Preparation

Preparation is crucial for the appraisal interview. It is essential that both you and your appraisee have at least ten days' notice of the meeting. This gives you both time to consider fully your own agendas.

You will have to set aside time to read last year's appraisal and think about the one in hand. In fact, you must make time to read all the relevant paperwork before structuring your interview. If your company uses a prepared form or online pro forma, this will give you an outline of what you should be working towards.

Useful documentation can include:

- previous appraisals
- job description
- performance standards
- notes from the year's events
- employee records
- reports from others
- training data
- examples to support feedback
- blank appraisal form
- appraisee's self-assessment
- appraisee's agenda.

Many companies also provide appraisees with a form on which they can make notes and consider their approach to the interview. The appraisee can return this to you before the interview if they wish, If you both have time, you can arrange a short meeting to discuss agenda items so that at the appraisal you both know what to expect and don't need to spend time negotiating.

No surprises

An appraisal is not a time for surprises. You will be discussing issues that have arisen throughout the year and including positives as well as areas for improvement. With appraisal in mind, you may have made notes since the last formal meeting of what you both said and did on significant occasions. You will need to refer to these before the interview.

Reports from others

If you are the appraisee's main manager, who else has relevant information about their work? You will need to talk to them before the interview. This can be time consuming, especially if there are any personality clashes. It is important here to collect facts and evidence regarding the appraisee's work behaviour rather than hearsay or unsubstantiated opinions. You may have to balance and make judgements about quite differing pictures of the same person.

Timing

You should both allow an hour and a half for the interview. This gives you some time after the appraisal to collect your thoughts and make any notes before returning to everyday work. If the interview runs for longer than an hour, it is worth thinking about arranging a follow up rather than slogging on to the bitter end. You will both be tired and cease to be effective.

As we saw on Monday, active listening involves a great deal of concentration. You may be surprised at how much energy you use. Remember this when you consider how many appraisals you would be able to handle in any one day. If you have more than a couple of staff to appraise, it would be a good idea to spread out your interviews over the year.

The interview

It is important to create a balanced interview. As well as recognizing and praising the appraisee's strengths, be clear about the areas for improvement. The appraisee should leave feeling positively challenged and that there has been an honest exchange of views and information.

Purpose

A good way to start the appraisal interview is to remind the appraisee why you are both there. It is likely that they are feeling apprehensive and uncertain, especially if this is their first appraisal with you or your company. This is an interview that is recorded and can affect their promotion and pay prospects. You have already clarified the purpose for yourself; now let them know. Emphasize that this is an opportunity for constructive dialogue and discussion. Let them know if you plan to make brief notes and suggest they can take some too.

Agenda

This may have already been arranged at a short meeting before the appraisal interview. You will both have topics that you want to cover and most will probably overlap. At this point, you need to outline the order you want to take and agree it.

Do you start with:

- the appraisee's areas for development/improvement?
- their strengths?
- appraisee's assessment of the above?
- competences and behaviours?
- goals attained, objectives achieved?

Do you follow:

- the appraisal form in strict order?
- the job description statement by statement?

When should you mention:

- next year's targets and objectives?
- training?
- personal development plans?

Whichever you decide, let the appraisee know. Keep an open mind and if the discussion goes out of sequence for a good reason, follow the flow.

Remember active listening from Monday. Make sure that you give your appraisee ample opportunity to convey their thoughts and ideas. You can aim for a ratio of them talking for 60 per cent of the time to your 40 per cent. Don't dominate the discussion.

Key areas to cover include:

- last year's appraisal and targets
- problems over the year
- successes over the year
- areas for improvement/training/development
- performance standards past/future
- areas of job dis/satisfaction
- agreed future targets.

Giving feedback

The most effective way to give and receive feedback is in an atmosphere of safety and trust. Remember, appraisal is a dialogue; if you have criticisms of an employee's work, be aware that they might also want to criticize you.

When giving feedback, remember to include:

- be specific
- behaviour/effects on others
- feelings
- their ideas/possible changes
- outcomes.

Be specific

Whether your feedback is positive or negative, it is best to refer to specific incidents you have observed or been told about. You want to encourage development and self-awareness in your appraisee. You will not do so by saying, 'that was great' or 'you were lousy'. Give clear examples, such as:

'I'd like to discuss your role on the safety committee; I am aware that the minutes are still taking over two weeks to be circulated.'

'Let's look at the last time the representative from Holland's was here...'

Behaviour/effect on others

Before offering a criticism, think about what part of their behaviour it is that you want to comment on. You either want someone to change for improvement or to continue with behaviour that is effective. You may also have something to say about the effect these behaviours have on others.

If you are suggesting change, then you need to be sure that it is something the appraisee is able to change. Comments like, 'If you'd had experience of an office fire you'd understand the urgency' are most unhelpful. Better to say something like: 'Decisions taken at the health and safety committee affect all staff. When you delay writing up the minutes, colleagues become anxious.'

Be clear when you are reinforcing the positives: 'I was pleased to see you listening to her, letting her finish what she was saying and then summarizing your agreed plan of action. She looked pleased too.'

Feelings

It is important to express how you feel about the situation. This can be a way of letting the appraisee know the strength of your criticism or praise. Use expressions such as:

'I was pleased...' '...and I'm delighted.'
'I feel increasingly annoyed when...' '...I was left feeling extremely uncomfortable.'

Their ideas/possible changes

These are key to the appraisal process. Your aim is to reach an agreement that is acceptable to both of you; this will be more successful than imposing your own ideas without discussion. Very often if you ask for an appraisee's ideas or suggestions for change, they will have plenty to say. After all, they will know about these matters as they have been dealing with them throughout the year. If you don't elicit their ideas, you will lose their commitment.

Outcomes

What are the possible consequences of the behaviour you are discussing? These can have a bearing on whether you reach an agreement about the need for change.

'It is vital that the minutes are circulated within 48 hours. If this doesn't happen, we will appear disinterested in safety issues.'

'If you continue to practise active listening, you'll find negotiating much easier.'

Receiving feedback

During the appraisal interview, you will be asking for comments from your appraisee and seeking their ideas for change. It is quite possible that some of these may include criticisms directed at you. *Listen* to what the appraisee is saying, and consider it carefully before responding. There may be something for you to learn too.

Receiving criticism

When receiving criticism, practise the following dos and don'ts.

Don't:

- deny the criticism
- become defensive
- argue
- sulk
- justify yourself.

Do:

- listen carefully
- ask for clarification
- decide whether the comment is valid
- consider what can be done, if the comment is true
- consider how this impression has come about, if the comment is not true/is partly true
- agree change
- consider what you have learned

Action plan and summary

Aim to have clear agreements of objectives and actions for the following year. The action plan should include review dates and success criteria. You will also want to confirm any development opportunities and their implementation.

Your summary will consist of a recap of any jointly agreed issues, agreed changes, development plans and areas of satisfaction. You can indicate what you will be including in the written appraisal document, and when you will be handing or mailing it to the appraisee for their comments and signature.

Whenever possible, aim to end the interview on a positive note even if you seem to be asking for a great many changes rather than encouraging them to keep up the good work. Remind them about the areas you are pleased with and emphasize that you have reached joint agreements in the areas for improvement. This is vital to ensure their commitment.

Follow up

Most companies require a formal record of the appraisal interview. Whether this is on a pre-designed form or left for you to organize, complete it as soon as you can after the interview. During the interview, you will have taken brief notes of the most important points. Immediately after the interview is the time to expand on them in greater detail. Be sure that any computerized information is secure and confidential.

Put into operation any agreements you reach with your appraisee. These could include organizing training, taking up coaching opportunities or arranging counselling. As soon as this process is completed, you can start collecting information for next year's appraisal.

Summary

Most people want to know how they are getting on at work. Even though you are talking to them throughout the year, the appraisal interview offers the chance to consider past and future projects in detail. The added bonus is that they have your complete and uninterrupted attention.

Checklist questions

- Will the interview be in your office, their office or a neutral meeting place?
- Have you agreed the date and time in advance?
- Have you collected and read all the relevant documentation?
- What is your agenda? How does it compare with theirs?
- What are the key areas for feedback – positives and areas for improvement?
- When will you summarize agreed actions?
- Can you deliver your promises and they theirs?

Effective appraisers are low on:

- putting forward their own ideas or solutions
- expressing opinions

- disagreeing/blocking
- interrupting
- commenting upon performance extremes.

Effective appraisers are high on:

- building/expanding others' ideas
- asking questions – feelings/facts
- listening – to test understanding/ summarizing
- seeking solutions
- evaluating – only when asked
- expressing feelings
- commenting on future performance.

And finally, appraisal is a great time to reinforce the praise you have been giving your staff over the year. Everyone needs praise, recognition and acknowledgement in their lives. Sometimes we seem to think that individuals should be psychologically strong enough to manage without it and should know their strengths without needing to be reminded. Or we worry that they will become big-headed and unbearable. In fact, encouragement and praise breed confidence, which enables others to take risks and expand their capacity at work. The more you give genuine praise, the better people will perform.

Questions (answers at the back)

1. Appraisal interviews are one part of performance management; others are:
   - a) 360-degree feedback ❏
   - b) Lunchtime chats ❏
   - c) Training programmes ❏
   - d) Away days ❏

2. Organizations benefit from appraisal interviews by:
   - a) Improved communications ❏
   - b) A stock-take of potential ❏
   - c) Better friendships between staff and managers ❏
   - d) Financial savings ❏

3. Managers benefit from appraisal interviews by:
   - a) Reinforced recognition and support for appraisee's work to date = increased motivation ❏
   - b) Opportunity to find out about appraisee's private life ❏
   - c) Discover appraisee's ambitions ❏
   - d) Practise interviewing skills ❏

4. Appraisees benefit from appraisal interviews by:
   - a) A change from their daily routine ❏
   - b) Gaining commitment for training ❏
   - c) A chance to offload a year's frustrations ❏
   - d) Improved morale and increased confidence ❏

5. In preparation for the appraisal interview, you will need:
   - a) The appraisee's holiday schedule ❏
   - b) Examples to support feedback ❏
   - c) Details of the appraisee's leisure interests ❏
   - d) Employee records ❏

6. Key areas to cover in an appraisal interview are:
   - a) Areas for improvement/ training/development ❏
   - b) Agreed future targets ❏
   - c) Last five years' appraisals ❏
   - d) Peer opinions of appraisee ❏

7. When giving feedback in an appraisal interview:
   - a) Only mention negatives ❏
   - b) Be specific ❏
   - c) Tell them what needs to change ❏
   - d) Invite their ideas for action ❏

8. When receiving feedback in an appraisal interview:
   - a) Listen fully to what is being said ❏
   - b) Argue your corner ❏
   - c) Decide whether the comment is true or untrue ❏
   - d) Ignore their ideas ❏

9. Effective appraisers are low on:
a) Expressing opinions ❏
b) Preparation ❏
c) Listening ❏
d) Interrupting ❏

10. Effective appraisers are high on:
a) Writing copious notes ❏
b) Using hearsay evidence ❏
c) Expressing feelings ❏
d) Checking and testing understanding ❏

THURSDAY

Coaching

Coaching has become a much more accepted and expected part of managing people since the first edition of this book. Many of the ideas for business coaching came initially from sports training techniques as it became clear that motivating staff is in many ways the same as motivating athletes. People learn and improve when they have a clear purpose and end in sight. One popular model for sports and business coaching is the GROW model.

G: Agree the GOAL or outcome to be achieved. Help your coachee define a goal that is specific, measurable and realistic.

R: Coachee considers their current REALITY. 'What is happening now and what learning or information is there in the present situation?'

O: Explore the OPTIONS. Help your coachee generate as many good options as possible, and discuss these. Offer your own suggestions, after your coachee has put forward theirs.

W: Establish the WILL. Help your coachee establish their will and motivation and be sure that they commit to specific action. 'So what will you do now, and when?'

Coaching is an ongoing part of a manager's workload, which, over time, will help you increase the motivation and effectiveness of your staff. The coaching process is likely to involve at least two interviews with a clear action element sandwiched in between. Unlike the formal appraisal interview, which usually occurs annually, coaching interviews occur throughout the working year. They are not performance management review interviews; they are part of your ongoing staff management responsibilities. They don't have to be formal, and indeed can be very successful when spontaneous.

In this chapter on coaching interviews, we will consider the following:

Purpose
Preparation
Opening interview
Follow up – review interview

Coaching is not to be confused with training. Training off the job involves going away to a classroom environment or working on distance learning packages before returning to implement the learning at work. On-the-job training involves 'sitting with Nellie' when someone is new to a task or organization. They first watch a colleague perform the operation before being observed as they take it on.

While training and coaching both promote learning, they do so in different ways:

- *Training* is about teaching specific skills or knowledge – *Coaching* is about facilitating someone else's thinking and helping them learn on the job.
- *Training* usually takes place off-site or in dedicated classes – *Coaching* takes place in the office and (when carried out by a manager) can be integrated into day-to-day workplace conversations.
- *Training* is more typically carried out in groups – *Coaching* is usually a one-to-one process, tailored to the individual's needs.

The key to coaching is that, after you have identified and agreed a learning opportunity, you leave the individual to perform the task alone. The role of the manager is to debrief thoroughly the staff member *before* and *after* the event.

You therefore have several options available to you, which are summarized in the following chart. You need to decide which is the best one; best for you, the manager, best for the organization and best for the coachee. All have a place in closing the gap between the standard required and present performance as well as helping the good become excellent.

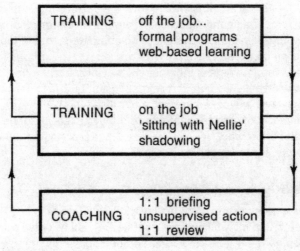

TRAINING	off the job... formal programs web-based learning
TRAINING	on the job 'sitting with Nellie' shadowing
COACHING	1:1 briefing unsupervised action 1:1 review

Adapted from Rapport CC

Purpose

Coaching interviews enable individual development in two distinct ways. Many companies only use coaching when mistakes are being made or when someone fails to reach the required standards. Its other application is to recognize potential and then empower employees to acknowledge their strengths and understand their accomplishments.

Coaching involves:

● improving poor performance
● building on competence and success.

Improving poor performance

When someone is clearly not reaching the agreed standards at work or is consistently repeating an error, they tend to be sent for training, and if that doesn't work, they are often disciplined. Coaching provides an interim measure for achieving the desired improvement. By spending time with the individual, you can work through the difficulties and agree a plan of action for them to follow. Then it is vital to arrange a review interview and assess what has happened. This is different from disciplining an employee because the underlying objective is that of looking for learning indicators from the experience.

For example: Chris is increasingly avoiding a particular customer whose account is her responsibility. A first coaching interview will explore why, involve her ideas in encouraging her to make contact and then let her do it. At the second interview, you can review what happened. This is better than just telling her to get out there and do her job.

Building on competence and success

This is where coaching comes into its own. By developing your staff and increasing their confidence, you will also be developing the organization and creating space for your own growth. You will be able to delegate more and so leave space to extend your competencies. Take great care to check that you are delegating meaningful tasks, not just dumping the ones you don't like.

Coaching increases:

- staff confidence and risk taking
- staff autonomy
- staff skills and abilities

- a sense of partnership between manager and staff
- job satisfaction.

It may be that you want to prepare an employee to take over when you are on leave, at a training course or need them to chair a meeting in your absence. You may assign someone to run a specific project or second them to another department. Each time you use such incidents as coaching opportunities, you will be enabling your staff to learn and understand their learning. By spending time with them in the short term, you will save time in the long term as their confidence to make decisions increases.

Preparation

In preparation for coaching, you need to:

- identify opportunities
- consider learning styles
- clarify objectives
- document what you have done.

Identify opportunities

If the organization is planning changes in procedure or staffing that will directly affect you and your team, then this will predetermine your coaching opportunities. In other instances, it is your responsibility to know your team's abilities and be looking for development opportunities. It may be that someone is expressing boredom or is clearly on top of all their responsibilities; this may be a case of preparing for promotion however far away that may be. Finally, you may have to act if someone is regularly making errors or not performing satisfactorily. In each case, there is a gap in performance or motivation that can be filled through coaching.

Consider learning styles

Before you enter into a coaching interview, think about the way your coachee likes, and is open to, learning. Learners can be broadly classified into four styles, and it is important to match the coaching interview to your coachee's preferred style. You will need to consider this beforehand to make most effective use of the interview.

The main learning types are:

- Activist: likes to learn by getting involved in projects straight away. Doesn't like to sit and watch. They are likely to say: 'I often act without considering the possible consequences', 'I actively seek new experiences'.
- Reflector: likes time to prepare and consider before action. Observes first and then performs. They are likely to say: 'I like time to prepare thoroughly', 'I'm always interested to find out what others think'.
- Theorist: likes to see systems, theories and models. Fits facts into theories for understanding. They are likely to say: 'I am often the most dispassionate and objective person in a discussion'.
- Pragmatist: likes to put practical application into ideas. Likes to experiment with new ideas. Concentrates on job-related issues. They are likely to say: 'What matters most is whether something works in practice'.

Many people favour just one of the styles, while some can adapt to two or three. If you can be alert to this before the opening interview, it is more likely to be successful. Just as activists do not like to sit through repetitious practice sessions, reflectors will not perform well if they are thrown in at the deep end without warning.

Consider your own learning style. It may be quite different from your coachee's, and this could affect your understanding in the coaching interview. Part of your preparation for the opening interview could well involve consciously putting aside how you would tackle things and being ready to listen to their approach.

Clarify objectives

Be clear about why you have taken this coaching opportunity. Consider how it will have an impact on the organization as well as the coachee and yourself. While you may be used to setting work goals with your staff, in the coaching interview you will be setting learning goals too. So, for Chris, who was avoiding contacting a customer (Green), the work goal would be regular contact with Green. The learning goal would be understanding and eliminating the anxieties that prevented it.

Take time to check that the goals you are aiming for are clear in your mind. They may change during the interview but you need to start with a specific task that is measurable and achievable while stretching for the coachee.

Documentation

Think about:

- Are there any papers or forms that the coachee will need to assist them with their task?
- Are there personal contacts they will need to make?
- What ideas/experience do you have to offer?
- Are there any legal requirements?

Always remembering that this is a chance for the coachee to establish their own learning, you can still have ideas and suggestions available if required.

SUNDAY MONDAY TUESDAY WEDNESDAY THURSDAY FRIDAY SATURDAY

Opening interview

The opening interview is the first bite of the coaching sandwich. This is where you discuss the task to be undertaken, elicit the coachee's ideas and help them consider any concerns. Whereas on Wednesday, in the appraisal interview, you were surveying the coachee's whole year, here you are working through one activity at a time.

Scene setting

This interview need not necessarily take place in your office. Depending on the layout of your workplace, it may be as easy to go to the coachee's workstation or office for the discussion. You will want to ensure that wherever you choose is comfortable for both of you, is conducive to good listening, and sufficiently private to avoid others' attention. It is a good idea to pick a time when you both can spare at least 20 minutes to guarantee a full dialogue. The ideal is a relaxed atmosphere and a shared knowledge that this is an important interview.

Encourage and enable

The coaching interview is definitely not a tell-sell interview. Your aim is to encourage the coachee to work out their own goals and the methods they choose to achieve them. There will of course be an element of control from you in the sense that you may initially influence the area to be worked on. You will also need to clarify the limits of their responsibility. What authority do they have, and what level of decisions can they make without referring to you?

As a manager you are used to devising and giving out instructions; as a coach, the emphasis changes to one of listening and support. This may seem strange at first and it is worth considering what can help or hinder that process.

Helping strategies:

- Give the coachee time to think through the issues. After all, you have prepared for this interview; they might not have thought about it before.
- Accept when the coachee has doubts about their ability. Rather than the all too common 'I know you can do it', acknowledge their concern and investigate it together: 'Tell me what's bothering you'.
- Encourage the coachee to put forward their own ideas and suggestions.
- Respect those ideas and listen with an open mind.
- Although not expecting mistakes, be clear that these will be accepted as learning opportunities, not something to be feared.
- Ensure that any special projects are seen to be worthwhile and useful to the organization, not just an excuse for keeping the coachee occupied.
- Be clear that you will stand back and let the coachee perform the agreed actions.

Unhelpful strategies:

- Avoid dependency caused by imposing solutions or being too quick to put your views forward.
- Don't dump routine tasks or ones you don't like.
- Take care not to become involved in or to provoke an argument.

- Refrain from smothering the coachee's attempts at showing initiative.
- Don't try to be too clever or use the interview to score points against the coachee.

Key questions

Questions checklist

- Elicit opinions on the task.
'What do you think about...? Have you considered...?'
'I've noticed... How do you see it?'
'What experiences have you had so far?'

- Discuss possible actions.
'How might you tackle it?'
'Who else do you need to involve?... When? What would you do first?... Second?'
'What is your timescale?'

- Consider pitfalls.
'What problems do you envisage? Have you thought about...?'
'Are there any obstacles that spring to mind?'

In the main, you will be concentrating on using the open questions we described on Monday. Your aim is to assist the coachee to work out their action plan and timetable as they see it. Part of your role in the interview is to check that they consider the subject from as many angles as possible. You want to encourage them to set themselves up for success not failure. Only put forward your own suggestions when you are sure the coachee has exhausted theirs.

And remember they are only suggestions...

Agree action

Make sure that you are both clear and in agreement about the action to be taken.

'Chris, you are going to phone Green on Wednesday afternoon and make an appointment to go through the account in person at a meeting to be arranged. You would like to visit their offices and see the system in operation. We have agreed tactics to cover the sarcasm you received before and you are happy, if a little bit nervous, to implement them if necessary.

We will meet on Wednesday week to discuss the outcomes.

How does that fit with your idea of what's next?'

If required, part of the coaching role may be to rehearse a situation during the opening interview. This way you can observe the coachee's current way of dealing with things, understand their concerns and increase their confidence.

Set a date and time to review their experiences – and make sure that you stick to it. Checking back is vital to ensuring that they have made the changes they are proposing – or if they haven't, to work out together what's stopped them.

Wait and see

This can be the hardest part of the coaching process. You are taking a risk when increasing someone's responsibilities, knowing that ultimately the buck stops at your door. If you have briefed them fully in the opening interview, you are most likely to be pleased with the outcome.

An added risk is that there is a chance they will perform better than you and may become a threat to your own position. This can explain the fear some managers have of delegation; that increasing another's expertise can endanger your prospects. This depends on the culture of the organization you work for. Where coaching is encouraged, then everyone is working towards greater autonomy in a supportive environment, not just your staff. In an authoritarian culture, you are unlikely to make much progress.

Follow up – review interview

This is an integral part of the coaching process, which you should not neglect. You will have arranged a date at the opening interview. This is your opportunity to assess together the learning and experience gained from the activity.

When reviewing the interview, you need to consider:

- self-assessment
- feedback
- what next?

Self-assessment

Resist the temptation to overwhelm the coachee with a list of strengths and limitations that you have observed or imagined may have occurred. Instead, assist them to develop self-assessment skills so that they can be more aware of their development needs. Many of us are quick to identify mistakes while dismissing our successes. It is up to you to help the coachee take a reasoned approach to both. You may want them to consider:

- What went well?
- What pleased you?
- What could you have done differently?
- Which were the challenges?
- What held you back?
- What facilitated you?

You are asking questions to help the coachee think through the issue and make their own decisions. Don't impose your own solutions and values.

Feedback

When you are both satisfied that you have covered the coachee's assessment, it is appropriate to give your own feedback. It may be worth spending a few minutes outlining your understanding of feedback and its purpose so as to avoid defensiveness or inertia. As we saw on Wednesday in the appraisal interview, this can be exceedingly helpful if given in a supportive and positive way. Your aim is to consolidate and confirm the new knowledge and skills gained by the coachee and to reinforce what they have done well.

Help them to consider that there is always learning behind any mistakes and that they can develop new improved strategies.

> *'The person who never made a mistake, never tried anything new.'*
>
> Einstein

What next?

There is no guaranteed outcome to a coaching interview. Much depends on the nature of the initial goals and actions. If everything has gone well, you may both want to consider further challenges for the coachee on an agreed structural basis. If the review interview throws up a basic operational problem, it may be that the coachee needs to go for more or first-time off-the-job training. If they are nearly there, but still lacking the confidence to act alone, you may want to send them back to 'Nellie' for a while. Whichever option you finally agree, be careful that you have approached it with an open mind after a thorough review.

Summary

The coaching interview enables you and the coachee to develop your existing skills in many different ways. You may be preparing them to deputize for you in the case of holidays, or letting them take more responsibility in one particular section of work. The more you coach effectively, the greater your capacity for self-improvement too.

Remember:

- Be on the lookout for coaching opportunities.
- Consider the coachee's learning style especially if it differs from yours.
- Use the GROW model to enhance successful outcomes.
- Listen to their ideas and suggestions before offering yours.
- Wait and see – don't interfere unnecessarily.
- Help them review and analyze their experiences – don't do it for them.

Telling team members that a job has been well done is an integral part of the coaching process. Most people need to feel wanted and coaching is a way of giving employees a confidence boost and faith in themselves.

SUNDAY
MONDAY
TUESDAY
WEDNESDAY
THURSDAY
FRIDAY
SATURDAY

In her book *Time to Think*, Nancy Kline suggests that: 'A five to one ratio of motivational to formative feedback helps people think for themselves.' Spot and take the opportunity to praise your coachees whenever you can. Don't assume or leave to chance the fact that they know they are making good progress. You probably feel you have to point out and respond to non-conformances and sometimes forget to spread positive messages too. Say it immediately in private or in public. Don't wait until the right time. It needn't be a great speech. Just let them know you've noticed and appreciated what they've done.

Coaching used to be just about performance. In the past few years, it has moved to include underlying motivations of personal fulfilment: the 'why' underneath the desire to achieve performance goals.

The keys to successful coaching are to believe in the potential of your people, raise their awareness, praise them, help them to help themselves take action and learn as they GROW.

Questions (answers at the back)

1. In a coaching interview, the G of the GROW model relates to:
   a) Gathering information ❑
   b) Setting goals ❑
   c) Agreeing actions ❑
   d) Agreeing outcomes ❑

2. In a coaching interview, the R of the GROW model relates to:
   a) Current reality ❑
   b) Setting realistic goals ❑
   c) Reminding the coachees of their targets ❑
   d) Utilizing the present scenario ❑

3. In a coaching interview, the O of the GROW model relates to:
   a) Clarifying outcomes ❑
   b) Considering options ❑
   c) Discussing available opportunities ❑
   d) Organizing an action plan ❑

4. In a coaching interview, the W of the GROW model relates to:
   a) Watching your coachee's progress ❑
   b) Waiting for the right time to intervene ❑
   c) Establishing the coachee's willingness to act ❑
   d) Ensuring the coachee's commitment to take action ❑

5. Coaching increases:
   a) Punctuality ❑
   b) Job satisfaction ❑
   c) Staff turnover ❑
   d) Confidence and risk taking ❑

6. If your coachee has an activist learning style, they will:
   a) Sit and observe before action ❑
   b) Want to get involved immediately ❑
   c) Work out all the options in advance ❑
   d) Shoot first and ask questions later ❑

7. If your coachee has a reflector learning style, they will:
   a) Want time to prepare and consider before action ❑
   b) Prefer to observe before they do ❑
   c) Require good clear explanations rather than practical opportunities ❑
   d) Like to experiment with new ideas ❑

8. If your coachee has a theorist learning style, they will:
   a) Be attracted to logically sound theories ❑
   b) Want to get involved immediately ❑
   c) Enjoy new challenges and experiences, and carrying out plans ❑
   d) Fit facts into theories for understanding ❑

9. If your coachee has a pragmatist learning style, they will:
a) Like to experiment with new ideas ❏
b) Prefer to observe before they do ❏
c) Be good at finding practical uses for ideas and theories ❏
d) Fit facts into theories for understanding ❏

10. What are the keys to successful coaching?
a) Regular and sincere praise ❏
b) Offering positive solutions ❏
c) Raising awareness ❏
d) Believing in your coachees ❏

FRIDAY

Counselling

It is hard to work efficiently when you're feeling stressed. Worry and loss of concentration can produce absenteeism and more inefficiency than machine down-time and yet many managers are better at getting machines fixed than helping their staff to deal effectively with emotional issues. If you have tried understanding someone who is facing a private crisis, then you will know that it can be challenging and uncomfortable. It can also be very rewarding. Using counselling skills, you can learn a practical, structured way of helping without taking over or becoming overwhelmed.

A recent HSE survey reported that an estimated average of 27 working days per affected case, or 10.8 million reported working days, are lost in the UK each year through stress-related illness. In today's demanding and fast moving business environment, the ability to manage pressure and deal with stress constructively is critical.

The counselling interview differs from those on the other days of the successful interviewing week because it may be initiated by your staff member rather than yourself. They might be the one to approach you and ask for some private time to talk about an issue that is about anything – work-related or outside work. Your job is to take off your manager's hat and use active listening to help them work through whatever is stressing them. Equally, you may recognize what you think are signs of stress in a team member or one of your staff. This could take the form of a change in their behaviour, attitude or appearance. You need to find an opportunity to invite them to talk to you. Be sure to *invite* them to talk to you and not compel them. If you try to force them to disclose all, you will only alienate them.

In looking at counselling interviews, we will cover:

General preparation
The interview
Follow up

A counselling interview is not a disciplinary interview. Your role is much more one of helper than manager. You are there to assist the counsellee come to terms with whatever is worrying them through understanding and acceptance.

General preparation

It is important to consider how you might handle a counselling interview. There is a good chance that you won't be able to prepare for each specific case, and no two cases are the same because of the individuality of those involved. If you have thought about the following guidelines, they will stand you in good stead. You are not expected to be a professional counsellor by the end of today, just someone more comfortable with issues of a personal nature.

General preparation includes looking at:

- the relationship
- confidentiality
- timing
- location.

The relationship

This is one instance where you have to quell your managerial instinct to tell someone what to do or find the solution to their problems. You have to remember that what they describe is their problem, not yours. Resist the temptation to take over the problem. This is one time when it is not appropriate to say, 'Leave it with me and I'll sort it out'. In a counselling relationship, you are initially providing a safe and private place for someone to discuss and think about issues that are affecting them at work, at home or both. You are not there as an expert or adviser, but as a concerned individual wanting to help them handle a difficulty or make a decision.

In the counselling relationship you:

● don't need specialist knowledge
● don't have to have all the answers
● don't take over their problems
● don't do it for them.

Central to the counselling relationship are three key attitudes that you will need to convey to your counsellee. Known as REG, they help to ensure a beneficial interview.

Key attitudes REG

Respect is:

● openness and acceptance of the counsellee
● suspending judgement and criticism
● considering that they are worth listening to.

Empathy is:

● understanding the counsellee's viewpoint
● putting yourself in their shoes
● understanding how they feel.

Genuineness is:

● a sincere interest in the counsellee
● being consistent and straightforward
● being yourself, not playing a role.

It takes courage to talk to a manager at work about personal issues, all the more so if the employee thinks they will be laughed at or belittled. REG enables you to concentrate on understanding, not judging. Carl Rogers, creator of person centre counselling, suggested that 75 per cent of what makes counselling work is the relationship of trust and unconditional acceptance demonstrated by using REG throughout the interview.

Confidentiality

This may well depend on the types of issues you are discussing. In most cases you will be discussing issues outside work, and will need to agree that the matters discussed go no further. If other staff are involved, you have to decide between the two of you whether to include those people in the conversation. Matters relating to health and safety might mean talking to a higher authority, and both you and the employee need to be clear about what is going to happen. Once someone has felt able to confide in you and been accepted, it is likely that they will know and agree if someone else needs to be brought in.

Take care not to breach confidentiality by treating the counsellee differently after a counselling interview because of your 'inside information'. Resist the temptation to make excuses for their behaviour or to cover up for them.

Comments like, 'If you knew what a time he's having with his teenager...' are a betrayal of confidence. You only need to break one confidence to become known as unreliable and untrustworthy.

Timing

If you have arranged the interview beforehand, you can ensure that you leave yourself at least 30 minutes, no more than an hour, for the session. Add ten minutes to reflect and initiate any agreed actions. Any longer than an hour will probably mean that you start to go over old ground. It is better to arrange a second interview than keep going until you both collapse. If you are approached without warning, you may not be able to put things on hold straight away. The minimum you should aim at is a few minutes to get an idea of the subject matter, and then an agreement to meet later at a mutually acceptable time. People can hold on to their concerns if they know you are interested and will be available when you say. If you try to tackle a counselling interview when you are busy thinking about your own work schedule, REG won't be with you and neither will you be with the employee.

Location

More than ever, location needs to be somewhere quiet and free from interruptions. If you work in a very busy office where people can see, if not hear, what you are doing, then you will have to take over someone else's office. You may have to go for a walk outside the building. It is not a good idea to go to a pub or social club as you can confuse roles and are in greater danger of breaching confidence. The counselling interview will only be successful in a private, unhurried and confidential setting. It is your responsibility to provide it.

The interview

The counselling interview can be divided into three stages. This is not a rigid structure and you will often move around the stages. Some counsellees will only need you for the first, listening stage; others may go to the second, while some may need all three.

Throughout the counselling interview, you will need to use the skills of active listening as described on Monday.

The three-stage model is based on 'The Skilled Helper' by Gerard Egan, which is a systematic way of working with another person to help them cope more effectively with their life. The model aims to provide that person with the skills required.

There is a pre-helping stage that stresses the importance of attending and listening.

The stages of the counselling interview

Pre-helping stage:

- Set the scene – think about the atmosphere you wish to create.
- Can you avoid interruptions?

Stage 1 Understanding

- What is the other person's story?
- How do they feel?
- Is there more than one concern?
- Let the other person know that you understand how they are affected.

Stage 2 Moving On

- Is there another way of looking at the situation?
- How might things look if your counsellee were managing them better?
- What is keeping them 'stuck' where they are?
- What do they need to do to make things different?

Stage 3 Action

- What practical help can you offer that they cannot do for themselves?
- What new skills do they need to learn and/or practise?
- How many realistic options are open to them?
- What are their goals?

Review and evaluation

Stage 1 Understanding

At the beginning of a counselling interview, give your full attention to understanding what the problem or issue really is. People often worry about things for ages before deciding to take the risk and talk about them, or before their behaviour means they are called to account. Once they start talking, you may have to sort out a jumble of emotions and ideas.

Your first task is to hold back and *listen* with undivided attention. You can expect to do about 80 per cent listening at this stage and only 20 per cent talking. This enables the counsellee to clarify their concerns. Don't write notes – the counsellee will be wary of what you might use the information for. Use *open* questions, paraphrasing, clarifying, encouraging responses and *REG* to enable the counsellee to start unpacking their story.

One aim of an effective counselling interview is to help the counsellee recognize and accept their feelings. Feelings are important and if they are not expressed they can restrict a person's ability to make decisions or choices. Most people are happier talking about their thoughts but they might need you to help them find the 'feeling' words.

Compare: 'I feel I would work better if there was some chance of promotion', with: 'I feel frustrated and stuck with career possibilities here'.

The first statement describes how the person is thinking about their performance, the second tells how they feel and is much more personally revealing. The opportunity to express feelings in a safe setting enables such feelings to be released and to lessen the anxiety so that the counsellee is able to think and eventually act more constructively.

It is very important in this stage to accept the counsellee's viewpoint and their feelings even if they are not the same as yours. If you start telling them how you would deal with things, they lose an opportunity to develop their own coping mechanisms. They may even feel further undermined if your solution is a simple one.

Resist the temptation to rush through Stage 1 at the cost of not fully exploring all the issues. The counsellee may start by talking about a safe subject before feeling able to talk about the more difficult concern.

Once clear about the problem, you can move on to Stage 2 if *they* want to. Just talking may have been enough. Some situations don't have a solution or easy answer. The skill then in Stage 1 is to give your counsellee time to talk. People will often thank you for just listening attentively when everyone else is full of ideas and answers.

Stage 2 Moving on

In this stage of the counselling interview, you will be helping the counsellee to see whether there are other ways of considering their dilemma. People sometimes get stuck in a particular thought pattern and believe there is only one way of looking at their situation. You can help the counsellee to explore alternatives and look for options. Even though you may be doing a little more of the talking in this stage of the interview, you still need REG to be with you.

Stage 2 skills in addition to stage 1 listening include:

● Feedback
'Perhaps people find it hard to take you seriously because you always laugh and play down your achievements.'

● Probing
'What would happen if you did that?'

● Challenging
'You said you wanted to work with someone else, and when we arranged the office move you didn't want to go. Where does that leave us?'

● Sharing your own experience
'I remember feeling very anxious the first time I had to speak to the directors. It gets easier.'

Be warned that this is not an excuse to start telling the counsellee about your problems. It is not a competition.

You need to have developed a trusting relationship to be able to challenge the counsellee in this stage of the interview. You are not trying to catch them out and show them up. They may be aware of the point you are making and still find it hard to accept. Give them time to think things through, avoid too much too quickly. Challenge carefully and with care. Your challenges will be more acceptable if you have REG with you.

At the end of Stage 2, you will have considered alternative ways of looking at the situation and various opportunities.

Stage 3 Action

Once the counsellee has considered all the options available to them, they may feel confident to go away and do whatever they see fit. However, they may still want you to help them put together an action plan. This involves helping them set realistic goals and not imposing your own solutions. As a manager, you are often expected to know what's best and see that it happens. In the counselling interview, your job is to help the counsellee come to their own conclusions. You need to help them work towards **manageable** targets. If their goal is enormous, like eating an elephant, the best way is to take one bite at a time.

Stage 3 skills in addition to stage 1 listening and stage 2 skills include:

● Goal setting: Make sure that the counsellee's goal is clear, specific and is attainable.
● Resourcing: You may be able to alter shifts, extend leave, arrange a transfer.
● Reviewing: Offer ongoing support to check progress, evaluate and possibly change goals over time.
● Referral: *Don't work outside your competence or comfort level.* Know when to stop and use outside agencies or your occupational health service. BACP will help you find a specialist agency or professionally qualified counsellor.

The British Association for Counselling & Psychotherapy (BACP) is a membership organization and a registered charity that sets standards for therapeutic practice and provides information for therapists, clients of therapy, and the general public.

As the largest professional body representing counselling and psychotherapy in the UK, BACP aim to increase public understanding of the benefits of counselling and psychotherapy, raise awareness of what can be expected from the process of therapy and promote education and/or training for counsellors and psychotherapists.

www.bacp.co.uk 01455 883300

Whatever help you offer in Stage 3, be sure to limit it to what the counsellee cannot do for themselves. Again resist the temptation to take over and 'get it sorted'.

Your contribution at this stage may include helping with a thorough examination of what may help or hinder the counsellee's chosen goal.

- Are there people who will aid or encourage the counsellee? (friends, colleagues, family)
- Are there situations that help or hinder? (working alone, with others, in a noisy atmosphere)

It is important to think these through and be prepared for any pitfalls.

Follow up

Unlike any of the other interviews that you conduct, there is no automatic follow up after the counselling interview. You will obviously go ahead and take any actions you agreed on the counsellee's behalf. You now need to act as though nothing has happened and put the counsellee's personal issues to one side. Destroy any notes you may have made or give them back to the counsellee.

You may want to arrange another discussion for a later date to check progress, as long as it's what the counsellee wants. This way, they know you are still interested in them and that it wasn't a one-off interview.

Continue watching for signs of personal problems that may be affecting your staff's performance and behaviour. Once they know you are approachable, you can deal with many issues before they are blown up out of proportion and are much harder to manage.

Summary

Counselling interviews are less likely to be planned than any of the other interviews. You have to expect the unexpected and be ready. You are not 'in-charge' of the counsellee but are more of a sounding board. Giving time to your counsellee when they need it can save time and crises later on.

There are some key differences between you counselling a staff member and them being referred to someone external: you are not a professional counsellor and don't have the benefit of the extensive training; you will know the counsellee and may have formed an opinion about them and their issue; they will know you and have opinions about you and your views of the world; confidentiality and its limits may be more of an issue – you have to continue working with them with the 'extra' knowledge you have.

Watch out too for the temptation to mind read and make assumptions about their issues, sometimes based on previous discussions with the person or on the basis of what you have 'heard'. Don't judge the other person; negative labels have enormous power. If you prejudge someone as childish

SUNDAY

MONDAY

TUESDAY

WEDNESDAY

THURSDAY

FRIDAY

SATURDAY

or boring, you won't pay much attention to what they say. You've already written them off. The basic rule of listening is that you shouldn't judge before you've heard the whole content of the message.

A counselling checklist

- Remember REG (Respect, Empathy, Genuineness).
- Give plenty of time to listening, especially in Stage 1 Understanding.
- Help the counsellee express their feelings.
- Notice who is doing most of the talking.
- Don't jump into problem-solving.
- You're not expected to have all the answers; there may not be any.
- Be clear about confidentiality.

Remember to take care of yourself too. A professional counsellor is expected to have regular supervision to counteract the stressors they encounter and to check that they are working in the most productive way with their counsellee. You may be listening to some strong emotions. Think about who you can talk to without breaking confidences. Otherwise you might be burdened by someone else's issues. Don't expect to be able to cope alone – otherwise you may end up as the next counselling case.

Questions (answers at the back)

1. Why might a counselling interview be different from the other interviews in the week?
a) They take longer ❏
b) There may not be any follow up ❏
c) They aren't work-related ❏
d) Your role is as a helper, not a manager ❏

2. Using your counselling skills, you are expected to:
a) Have all the answers ❏
b) Take over their problems ❏
c) Provide a safe and private place ❏
d) Curb the temptation to find the solutions ❏

3. In a counselling interview, the R in REG stands for:
a) Rationality ❏
b) Remembering ❏
c) Respect ❏
d) Openness ❏

4. In a counselling interview, the E in REG stands for:
a) Evaluation ❏
b) Empathy ❏
c) Understanding ❏
d) Eloquence ❏

5. In a counselling interview, the G in REG stands for:
a) Genuineness ❏
b) Graciousness ❏
c) Sincerity ❏
d) Gratitude ❏

6. In a counselling interview, take care not to breach confidentiality by:
a) Over-protecting on the basis of knowledge gleaned from the interview ❏
b) Dropping hints about your staff member ❏
c) Refusing to answer questions about their personal life ❏
d) Going to another manager behind their back ❏

7. The best pace to hold a counselling interview is:
a) The park ❏
b) The pub ❏
c) The canteen ❏
d) A meeting room ❏

8. In stage 1 of a counselling interview, you are:
a) Understanding ❏
b) Discovering their story ❏
c) Moving them to action ❏
d) Looking for alternative ideas ❏

9. In stage 2 of a counselling interview, you are:
a) Setting tasks ❏
b) Moving on ❏
c) Challenging ❏
d) Doing most of the listening ❏

10. In stage 3 of a counselling interview, you are:
a) Setting goals ❏
b) Giving feedback ❏
c) Probing ❏
d) Checking reality ❏

SATURDAY

Discipline

In order to operate effectively, organizations need to set standards of performance and conduct reinforced by company rules. Problems when standards are not met should first be addressed informally between manager and employee. In this way, the issues can be explored and a way forward agreed. However, if this fails or the problem is too serious, a formal approach may need to be adopted – one that helps employers to be fair and consistent.

Many managers and supervisors are apprehensive about discipline. They let small incidents go unchecked rather than tackling situations as they arise. The result may be loss of respect from staff and difficulties with senior managers when the situation eventually has to be handled. The longer you leave an issue, the more complicated it can become and the more of your time it is likely to take. Disciplinary procedures should be seen as an aid to effective management, to be used primarily as a means of modifying people's behaviour in line with the organization's aims – not just as a mechanism for imposing sanctions; this way, they are likely to be deemed less daunting.

In looking at disciplinary interviews, we will cover:

Company policy
Preparation
The interview
Interview dos and don'ts

Company policy

Your organization should have a discipline code or set of rules that are available to all staff. Disciplinary procedures may be used for issues with employees' conduct or performance, although some organizations have a separate procedure for dealing with performance problems.

Minor acts of misconduct include: poor timekeeping, unreasonable or unexplained absence, persistent or irregular absenteeism, minor damage to an employer's property, smoking in no-smoking areas, use of obscene or offensive language and so on.

Acts that constitute gross misconduct can include: theft, physical assault, breach of duty of confidentiality, sexual or racial harassment, fighting, wilful damage to an employer's property, sale and/or consumption of alcohol or drugs at work or being under the influence of alcohol or drugs at work, and failure to comply with lawful and reasonable instructions. It is helpful to have a non-exclusive list of examples of both types of misconduct in the organization's disciplinary procedure.

You need to be familiar with them and know how far your responsibility goes. Are you only expected to carry out the first informal interview or do you have the authority to go right to the end, culminating in dismissal if necessary?

There should also be established procedures for discipline, though sometimes these only relate to formal disciplinary interviews. If you don't adhere to the procedures set out, you could damage your case if it were to go to a tribunal. Where there is no existing procedure, check with colleagues for guidance and to see what has happened before. It is also important to find out the various stages of discipline that your company follows. You may want to contact Acas, whose code of practice sets out useful and well-tested ground rules. They also provide guidance on disciplinary practice and procedures and grievance procedures.

Acas

'Acas stands for Advisory, Conciliation and Arbitration Service. We aim to improve organizations and working life through better employment relations. We help with employment relations by supplying up-to-date information, independent advice and high quality training, and working with employers and employees to solve problems and improve performance.

Whether you're an employer or an employee you can get free advice from this website or by calling our telephone helpline. Employers might also be interested in our more specialized services, including training, workplace projects, conciliation and mediation.'

www.acas.org.uk

Preparation

Preparation is crucial for the disciplinary interview. It is vital that as many facts as possible are collected, whatever the level of formality.

Purpose

Why are you holding this interview? In the case of the formal disciplinary interview, it may be the last in a line of procedures that lead to terminating the interviewee's employment. Less formal interviews often represent an attempt to improve performance or standards so that the interviewee accepts the need for change and remains with the company. In some cases, the interviewee may be hampered by matters beyond their control and if so, you need to know about it. Then the disciplinary interview serves to eliminate the problem, not just to castigate the interviewee. Generally, your aim will be to detect and manage the situation before it leads to dismissal.

Information

Whatever the stage of discipline, you will need to have collected as much information as possible. Make sure that it is clear and specifically relates to the situation.

Information gathering can include:

- records – timekeeping, attendance, sales, performance statistics
- paperwork – previous interviews, reports from other managers, warning letters
- people – witnesses, other employees, colleagues, customers' complaints, suppliers' complaints (written allegations from complainant).

You would not expect to gain information from all these sources each time. Whatever you do collect, make sure that it is relevant and dated, and itemize it in note form for the interview.

In some instances, you will not have hard evidence to support a complaint. However, it is still important to continue with the interview and give the interviewee a chance to express their assessment of the situation.

A full investigation will take some time to organize. If there is any health, safety or security risk to the company or employees (fighting, drunk in charge of machinery, etc.) those concerned should be suspended on full pay until the disciplinary interview.

Notes

Make clear and specific notes for each item you wish to cover.
You should indicate the positive aspects of the interviewee's
work as well when it is appropriate. Be clear that if only
one section of an otherwise effective workload is causing
difficulties that this is presented in context.

> ### Example: Alec
> - response to phone calls: complaints from other depts.
>   of bored, offhand approach, hope Alec won't answer
> - very skilled researcher, concise written reports,
>   delivers data on time
> - problems with telephone technique?
> - responding to others interferes with 'his work'?

Have all your points listed so that you can go through and
check them off as you conduct the interview.

Notice

You may choose a quick informal interview there and then if
you happen to be on site as an incident occurs. Otherwise, you
will need to give the interviewee notice that you want to speak
with them. They need time to prepare themselves and any
presentation they wish to make. Depending on the formality
of the forthcoming interview, you may both wish to have
observers who will also need notice of the meeting.

Timing

Consider how you think the interviewee will respond in the
interview. If they are likely to be very upset or angry, it may
be wise to set the interview at the end of a day, a shift or even
a week. That way they can go home without having to face
colleagues, customers or machinery.

The interview

There are a number of points along the disciplinary continuum where it is appropriate to hold an interview. Whether you are engaged at the very informal or most formal stage of the process, you must endeavour to hold the interview in private. You are not aiming to humiliate the interviewee in front of customers or workmates; there is a chance that they will join in too. This could prejudice the outcome of the interview. In considering the interview, you need to think about:

- type of interview
- procedure
- notes.

Type of interview

The type of interview you are likely to hold will depend on the circumstances and seriousness of each case. You need to be clear with yourself and the employee at which stage of the disciplinary procedure you are operating.

Type of interview:

- On the job: clear-cut, minor misconduct. Instant verbal censure and indicate organization limits exceeded. Agree change required.

- Informal first and subsequent: prior notice of interview date and subject.
- Formal: prior notice of interview date, subject and relevant paperwork, plus observers.

Procedure

The procedure you will follow is very similar for each type of disciplinary interview, with the main difference being the involvement of other people as observers or witnesses.

The procedure should be:

- Outline subjects for discussion.
- Recap previous action taken if relevant.
- Role of observers.
- Allow interviewee time to explain.
- Consider interviewee's responses.
- Joint or interviewer-only solution.
- Summary, action plan and consequences.
- Agree review meeting.

Role of observers

This will depend on the disciplinary procedure that your company follows. At a formal interview, you will want someone to take notes and possibly to help you keep on track with the interview. The interviewee has the right to bring a colleague or a trade union representative if they wish. You all need to be absolutely clear whether this is for silent, moral support or in a speaking role.

In a first, informal, interview it may be more appropriate to hold the discussion between the two of you, indicating that unless the situation changes you will initiate more formal procedures. Consult your company policy; it may require observers from the start. Record the interview and have the interviewee sign in case of recurrence.

Allow the interviewee time to explain

The interview enables two-way discussion. There could be many reasons for the interviewee not working or behaving satisfactorily. You need to check that your facts and context are correct, giving them plenty of space to explain any extenuating circumstances relevant to the case.

Consider the interviewee's responses

It is possible that, having heard the interviewee's side of the story, you may decide to abandon the disciplinary interview in favour of a discussion about coaching, training or moving into counselling mode.

- Are they entirely to blame?
- Were there mitigating circumstances?
- Is someone else in the company responsible?
- Was there an organizational failure?
- Are these acceptable explanations or excuses?

You may need to adjourn the interview to investigate the new circumstances and to reassess the situation considering the interviewee's statements. You may already have some ideas about the improvements you require but these must be flexible to allow for the interviewee's input. Remember that you are looking for ways to achieve progress rather than dismissal. Dismissal is usually going to be your final sanction and last resort.

Summary, action plan and consequences

At the end of any disciplinary interview, summarize the discussion and the decisions reached. This ensures that you

can check all your points have been covered and can confirm
the agreed actions. Divide the action plan into steps to be
taken with the required timescale. See that the interviewee and
all relevant people have a copy.

Summarize:

- the subject discussed and why it is not acceptable
- interviewee's explanation
- mutual benefits of agreed change
- agreed actions and timings
- next step of discipline if no change.

Agree review meeting

Specify the time limits for the agreed changes and
improvement. No further disciplinary action should be
necessary during that time unless the interviewee has shown
no inclination to change. Hold regular progress checks to
monitor behaviour and performance.

If there has been only qualified improvement, you may
want to increase the time allowed. If the interviewee has
made satisfactory improvements, it is important that you
acknowledge and praise their success. For example:

'We've been discussing your attitude to information
requests made over the phone. We have agreed that your
responses of swearing and slamming the phone down are
not acceptable. I understand that the main problem is having

your concentration disturbed and that it takes a long time to reorganize your thoughts.

We have agreed that you will circulate a memo with both our signatures suggesting that telephone enquiries are acceptable before 9.30 and after 16.30. Where this is not possible, you would prefer email requests for information.

You are going to work at curbing your temper should calls be made outside the requested time.

We have also agreed to meet in a month's time to assess the situation.'

Notes

For the on-the-job interview, you can make a brief note to record the fact that you have spoken to the interviewee.

- employee – Jo Smith
- date – 10.03.2012
- reason for warning – timekeeping
- your signature.

The more formal interviews will require details of the contents of the interviews and the deadlines for action. Give a copy to the interviewee as soon as possible after the interview as well as keeping one on file. Depending on your company policy, there may be a requirement for you both to sign and agree as accurate a written record of the interview.

- employee
- date
- reason for interview
- interviewee responses
- actions to be implemented
- timescale
- next step if action not observed/maintained
- signature: interviewee
- signature: interviewer.

In the case of an appeal within the company or to an external arbiter, you will need comprehensive notes to show that you have correctly followed the required procedures.

Interview dos and don'ts

Do:

- ensure no interruptions from people, emails or texts
- convey appropriate formality
- allow for nerves on both sides – offer refreshment
- maintain regular eye contact with interviewee
- avoid raising your voice, physical contact
- keep as relaxed as possible to facilitate listening
- state the issues clearly and specifically with examples
- be consistent in all staff discipline.

Don't:

- get involved in arguments or defensiveness
- use the opportunity to throw every possible complaint at the interviewee
- make personal remarks
- resort to sarcasm.

Summary

You may not have to conduct many disciplinary interviews, but you should still take time to prepare yourself fully and be aware of your company's procedure just in case you are called upon.

Key questions

- Is there a company policy? Do you know it or how to access it?
- Who or what can help you prepare your case?
- Are you clear about the areas of complaint or dissatisfaction?
- What evidence can you collect? Where/who from?
- What specific and realistic changes do you want?
- Are there possible alternatives?
- Do both parties know which stage of the disciplinary process this is?
- Do either of you require observers?
- Have you informed the employee in writing of the reasons why they are having an interview, the time and place, and who will be present?
- Have you listened fully to the interviewee's case?
- What are the various consequences?
- Have you completed required paperwork?
- What are the next steps?

Procedural dos and don'ts

Do:

- gather all the facts before the interview
- leave enough time for both sides to prepare for the interview
- make the interview a discussion; let the employee have their say and listen to it
- record the evidence, the minutes of the interview and the outcomes
- inform the employee in writing of the action to be taken; both parties should then sign this.

Don't:

- neglect to check the organization's disciplinary procedure
- assume guilt before the interview
- finish the interview without setting clear goals for the future
- close without an agreed review date.

Make sure that you are clear about your organization's policy and procedures. Regularly visit the Acas website for any changes in the law and as a general resource for all matters to do with discipline and grievance procedures.

A note from the Acas website suggests:

'Whenever a disciplinary or grievance process is being followed it is important to deal with issues fairly. There are a number of elements to this:

- Employers and employees should raise and deal with issues promptly and should not unreasonably delay meetings, decisions or confirmation of those decisions.
- Employers and employees should act consistently.
- Employers should carry out any necessary investigations, to establish the facts of the case.
- Employers should inform employees of the basis of the problem and give them an opportunity to put their case in response before any decisions are made.
- Employers should allow employees to be accompanied at any formal disciplinary or grievance meeting.
- Employers should allow an employee to appeal against any formal decision made.'

Questions (answers at the back)

1. Disciplinary procedures are:
a) For dismissing staff ❏
b) An aid to effective management ❏
c) A means of modifying people's behaviour ❏
d) Always informal ❏

2. Minor acts of misconduct can include:
a) Substance abuse ❏
b) Unreasonable or unexplained absence ❏
c) Persistent or irregular absenteeism ❏
d) Vandalism ❏

3. Acts that constitute gross misconduct can include:
a) Use of obscene or offensive language ❏
b) Poor timekeeping ❏
c) Sexual or racial harassment ❏
d) Fighting ❏

4. The Advisory, Conciliation and Arbitration Service (Acas):
a) Supplies up-to-date employee relations information ❏
b) Provides legal aid ❏
c) Helps with conciliation and mediation ❏
d) Only advises employers ❏

5. You can collect information for a disciplinary interview from:
a) Colleagues ❏
b) Previous interviews ❏
c) Performance statistics ❏
d) Overheard conversations ❏

6. Disciplinary interviews can be:
a) On site as an incident occurs ❏
b) Formal and requiring prior notice ❏
c) Informal without any notice ❏
d) Conducted via an intermediary ❏

7. Included in the procedure for disciplinary interviews are:
a) Question and answer session ❏
b) Action planning ❏
c) Employer only input ❏
d) Set up review meeting ❏

8. What questions might you consider when listening to the interviewee's responses:
a) Were they let down by the organization? ❏
b) Am I interviewing the right person? ❏
c) Should I offer them a lie detector test? ❏
d) Is this a disciplinary issue? ❏

9. To make the disciplinary interview most successful:
a) Avoid raising your voice ❏
b) Make the interview as short as possible ❏
c) Don't make personal remarks ❏
d) Invite as many people as possible to attend ❏

10. Key questions you might want to ask before your disciplinary interview are:

a) What is the organization's disciplinary policy? ❏

b) Should the details of the interview be covered in the staff newsletter? ❏

c) Do you know the consequences of any proposed actions? ❏

d) Where and from whom can you collect evidence? ❏

Surviving in tough times

The interviewing guidelines and techniques covered in this book have given you an insight into the way successful interviews are created. Whether you're involved in selection, appraisal or coaching interviews, or being called on to implement counselling and disciplinary interviews, successful interviewing is an integral part of managing people. Planning and preparation are essential, and in these tough economic times it is more important than ever to take charge of the process and make the 'right' decision. Here, then, are ten crucial tips to help you.

1 Have clear objectives

What are your objectives? Be clear about what you're hoping to achieve from the interview. This will help you to prepare for and structure the interview, and to assess your success afterwards. Don't forget to let the interviewee know your objectives so that they have a chance to prepare appropriately too – they're not mind readers!

2 Prepare!

Preparation is the key to successful interviewing. Use positive self-talk to direct your energy towards effective preparation and to enhance your own performance. Make a list of all the documents needed for the interview and aim to read through them – if time is short prioritize your reading. Think about the organizational preparation for the interview: the interview structure (the stages you intend to follow), scene setting (the location of the room and the way it's set out) and administrative arrangements (timing, avoiding interruptions, limiting the number of interviews in one day).

3 Beware prejudice and bias

We can make decisions about a person or the outcome of an interview in a very short time, so you need to check whether you're relying on 'instincts' or assumptions rather than the facts. Your prejudices can lead to an outcome that you predicted and subconsciously encouraged. Concentrate on the whole picture, not just the parts that impress or disappoint you.

4 Build rapport

It is your task to create a positive connection during an interview. Rapport is demonstrated in many ways, including active listening and body language. To be an active listener is to be an effective listener, and you should expect to be listening much more than speaking when interviewing. Try using skills such as paraphrasing and clarifying to show that you really are listening to your interviewee. When you are speaking, remember SHEP: *Sound, Habits, Eye contact, Posture.*

5 Remember it's a matching process

When recruiting, you and your business will probably have invested a significant amount of time in the planning process before the interviewee is actually in front of you. In challenging economic times you can't afford to waste that time, so in the interview remember your key objectives and questions. Can they *do* the job? Do they *match* their CV data? Can they demonstrate that they have the *skills and experience* and do they *fit* your competency needs? The interviewee also uses the interview to assess how you and the company match their needs and expectations.

6 Use appraisals well

Most people want to know how they are getting on at work, and the appraisal interview offers the chance to consider past and future projects in detail. Remember an appraisal interview is an opportunity to mobilize the energy of every employee towards the achievement of strategic goals. Appraisal is also a great time to reinforce praise – encouragement and praise breed confidence and better performance!

7 GROW!

Coaching is an ongoing part of a manager's workload. Most people need to feel wanted and coaching is a way of giving employees a confidence boost and faith in themselves, which in turn increases motivation and commitment to the company – valuable at any time. Help them to GROW: agree the *Goal*; coachee considers their current *Reality*; explore the *Options*; establish the *Will*.

8 Take off your manager's hat

Worry and loss of concentration can produce absenteeism and more inefficiency than machine down-time, yet many managers are better at getting machines fixed than helping their staff deal with emotional issues. Using counselling skills, you can learn to help without taking over or becoming overwhelmed. Expect the unexpected and be ready to act as a sounding board – giving time to your counsellee when they need it can save time and crises later on. Remember REG: *Respect, Empathy, Genuineness*.

9 Don't be apprehensive about discipline

Tackle situations as they arise. The longer you leave an issue, the more complicated it can become and the more of your time it's likely to take. Think of disciplinary procedures as an aid to effective management, as a means of modifying people's behaviour in line with the organization's aims. Visit the Acas website regularly for any changes in the law and as a general resource for matters to do with discipline and grievance procedures.

10 Review and evaluate

Your final task after conducting any interview is to review how the interview went, what actions you have committed to and what you have learned from the session. Give yourself time to go back over the interview and assess your performance. Was the outcome satisfactory? Was your preparation appropriate? What would you do differently next time?

Answers

Sunday: 1a,b; 2a,c; 3a,b,c; 4a,c;
5a,b; 6b,d; 7a,d; 8c,d; 9b,d;
10a,d

Monday: 1a,c; 2b,c; 3a,d; 4a,c;
5c; 6b,d; 7a,b,d; 8a,d; 9a,b;
10a,d

Tuesday: 1a,d; 2b,d; 3c,d; 4a,c,d;
5a,c; 6a,c; 7c,d; 8a,b; 9b,c;
10a,b,d

Wednesday: 1a,c; 2a,b; 3a,c;
4b,d; 5b,d; 6a,b; 7b,d; 8a,c;
9a,d; 10c,d

Thursday: 1b,d; 2a,d; 3b,c; 4c,d;
5b,d; 6b,d; 7a,b, 8a,d; 9a,c;
10a,c,d

Friday: 1b,d; 2c,d; 3c; 4b; 5a;
6b,c,d; 7d; 8a,b; 9b,c; 10a,d

Saturday: 1b,c; 2b,c; 3c,d; 4a,c;
5a,b,c; 6a,b; 7b,d; 8a,b; 9a,c;
10a,c,d